W9-AYN-152

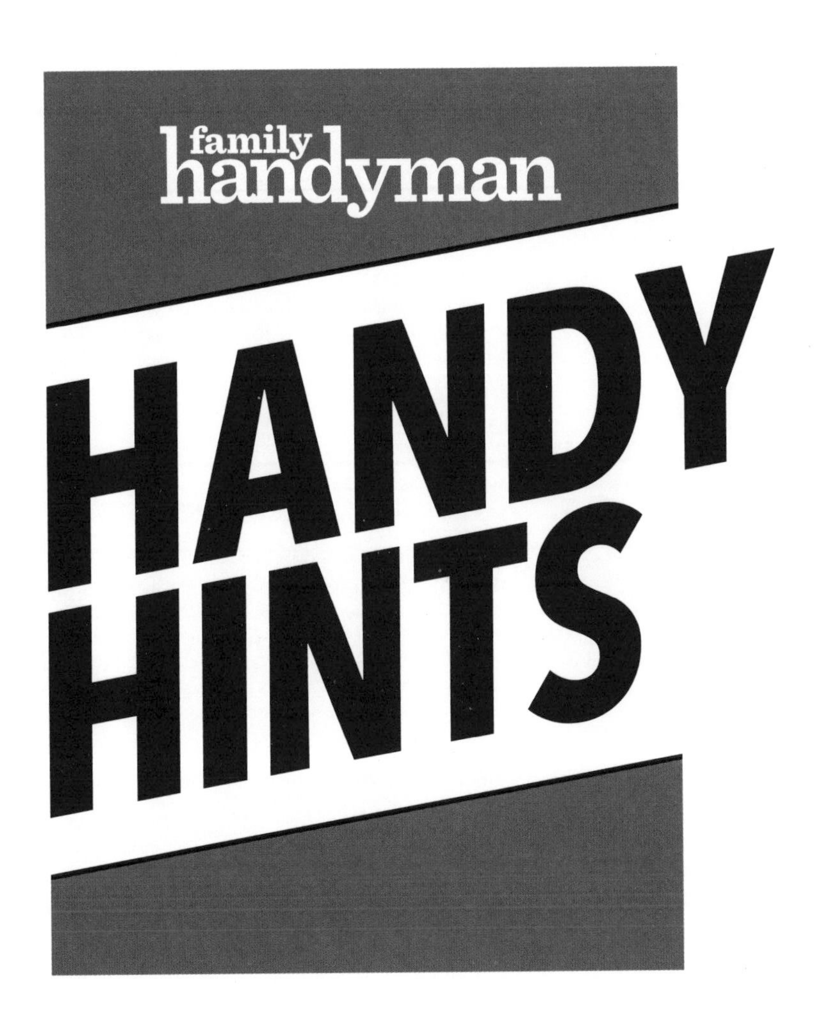
family handyman
HANDY HINTS

Text, photography and illustrations for *Family Handyman Handy Hints* are based on articles previously published in *Family Handyman* magazine (2915 Commers Dr., Suite 700, Eagan, MN 55121, familyhandyman.com).
For information on advertising in *Family Handyman* magazine, call 646-518-4215.



**PHOTOGRAPHY CREDITS**
**Images: 36, 52, 55, 71, 220** Mark Hardy; **39** Ruth Kallen; **40** Heath Donnald; **44** Karen Merkel; **54** Charles Wagner; **56** Bill Wells; **61, 161** Frank Rohrbach III; **87** Casey Hankins; **115** Ron Chamberlain; **147** Stephen Rusk; **153** Galen Lesher; **192** Chuck Bemben; **200** Bill Remia; **202** Dick Seils; **206** Kelley Griswold; **214** Mike Stackhouse; **218** Cody McGee; **219** Dave Early
**Getty Images: Chapter openers/hexagon pattern** carduus
**Shutterstock: 26** Natali_Mis

All other photographs by Jim Erickson, Tom Fenenga, Mike Krivit, Will Leighton, Ramon Moreno and Bill Zuehlke

Hardcover ISBN: 978-1-62145-776-3
Paperback ISBN: 978-1-62145-777-0
ePub ISBN: 978-1-62145-778-7
Component number: 119100104H
LOCC: 2021938423

**A NOTE TO OUR READERS**
All do-it-yourself activities involve a degree of risk. Skills, materials, tools and site conditions vary widely. Although the editors have made every effort to ensure accuracy, the reader remains responsible for the selection and use of tools, materials and methods. Always obey local codes and laws, follow manufacturer instructions and observe safety precautions.

PRINTED IN CHINA
1 3 5 7 9 10 8 6 4 2

# SAFETY FIRST—ALWAYS!

Tackling home improvement projects and repairs can be endlessly rewarding. But as most of us know, with the rewards come risks. DIYers use chain saws, climb ladders, and tear into walls that can contain big and hazardous surprises.

The good news is that armed with the right knowledge, tools and procedures, homeowners can minimize risk. As you go about your projects and repairs, stay alert for these hazards:

### ALUMINUM WIRING

Aluminum wiring, installed in about 7 million homes between 1965 and 1973, requires special techniques and materials to make safe connections. This wiring is dull gray, not the dull orange characteristic of copper. Hire a licensed electrician certified to work with it. For more information, go to *cpsc.gov* and search for "aluminum wiring."

### SPONTANEOUS COMBUSTION

Rags saturated with oil finishes like Danish oil and linseed oil, and oil-based paints and stains can spontaneously combust if left bunched up. Always dry them outdoors, spread out loosely. When the oil has thoroughly dried, you can safely throw them in the trash.

### VISION AND HEARING PROTECTION

Safety glasses or goggles should be worn whenever you're working on DIY projects that involve chemicals, dust, and anything that could shatter or chip off and hit your eye. Sounds louder than 80 decibels (dB) are considered potentially dangerous. Sound levels from a lawn mower can be 90 dB, and shop tools and chain saws can be 90 to 100 dB.

### LEAD PAINT

If your home was built before 1979, it may contain lead paint, which is a serious health hazard, especially for children ages 6 and under. Take precautions when you scrape or remove it. Contact your public health department for detailed safety information or call 800-424-LEAD (5323) to receive an information pamphlet. Or visit *epa.gov/lead.*

### BURIED UTILITIES

A few days before you dig in your yard, have your underground water, gas and electrical lines marked. Just call 811 or go to *call811.com*.

### SMOKE AND CARBON MONOXIDE (CO) ALARMS

The risk of dying in reported home structure fires is cut in half in homes with working smoke alarms. Test your smoke alarms every month, replace batteries as necessary and replace units that are more than 10 years old. As you make your home more energy-efficient and airtight, existing ducts and chimneys can't always successfully vent combustion gases, including potentially deadly carbon monoxide (CO). Install a UL-listed CO detector, and test your CO and smoke alarms at the same time.

### FIVE-GALLON BUCKETS AND WINDOW COVERING CORDS

Anywhere from 10 to 40 children a year drown in 5-gallon buckets, according to the U.S. Consumer Products Safety Commission. Always store them upside down and store those containing liquid with the covers securely snapped.

According to Parents for Window Blind Safety, hundreds of children in the United States are injured every year after becoming entangled in looped window treatment cords. For more information, visit *pfwbs.org*.

### WORKING UP HIGH

If you have to get up on your roof to do a repair or installation, always install roof brackets and wear a roof harness.

### ASBESTOS

Texture sprayed on ceilings before 1978, adhesives and tiles for vinyl and asphalt floors before 1980, and vermiculite insulation (with gray granules) all may contain asbestos. Other building materials made between 1940 and 1980 could also contain asbestos. If you suspect that materials you're removing or working around contain asbestos, contact your health department or visit *epa.gov/asbestos* for information.

**FOR ADDITIONAL INFORMATION ABOUT HOME SAFETY, VISIT *HOMESAFETYCOUNCIL.ORG*. THIS SITE OFFERS HELPFUL INFORMATION ABOUT DOZENS OF HOME SAFETY ISSUES.**

# CONTENTS

# CHAPTER 1

# CLEANING

bounce

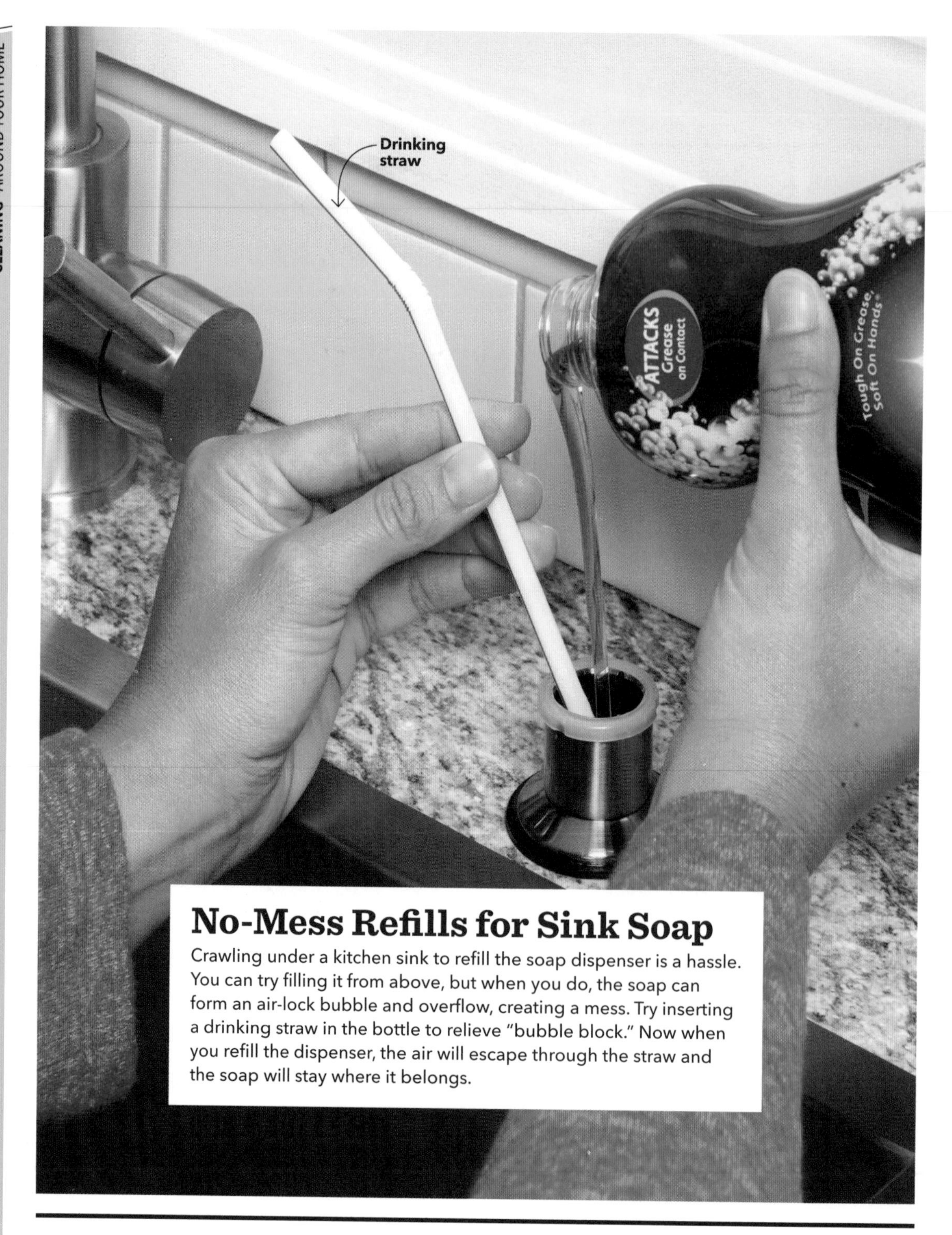


# No-Mess Refills for Sink Soap

Crawling under a kitchen sink to refill the soap dispenser is a hassle. You can try filling it from above, but when you do, the soap can form an air-lock bubble and overflow, creating a mess. Try inserting a drinking straw in the bottle to relieve "bubble block." Now when you refill the dispenser, the air will escape through the straw and the soap will stay where it belongs.

# MAGIC POULTICE FOR OIL-STAINED GROUT

If your tiled kitchen countertops and floor look terrible because of grease stains in the grout, and you think you've tried everything to get them out, try this two-step solution. First, make a thick paste of baking soda and water, and spoon it over the oil stains. Tape plastic over it and let it sit for 24 hours. Then make slits in the plastic and let the paste dry until there's no more moisture left (another 24 hours). Remove the plastic, sweep away the baking soda and voilà–clean grout!

## SPARKLING DISHWASHER

Once a month or so, add a cup of vinegar to your empty dishwasher and let it run a full cycle. Your kitchen may smell a bit like a pickle jar for a few hours, but hard-water lime buildup will be rinsed away, making your spray arm and other dishwasher parts work flawlessly.

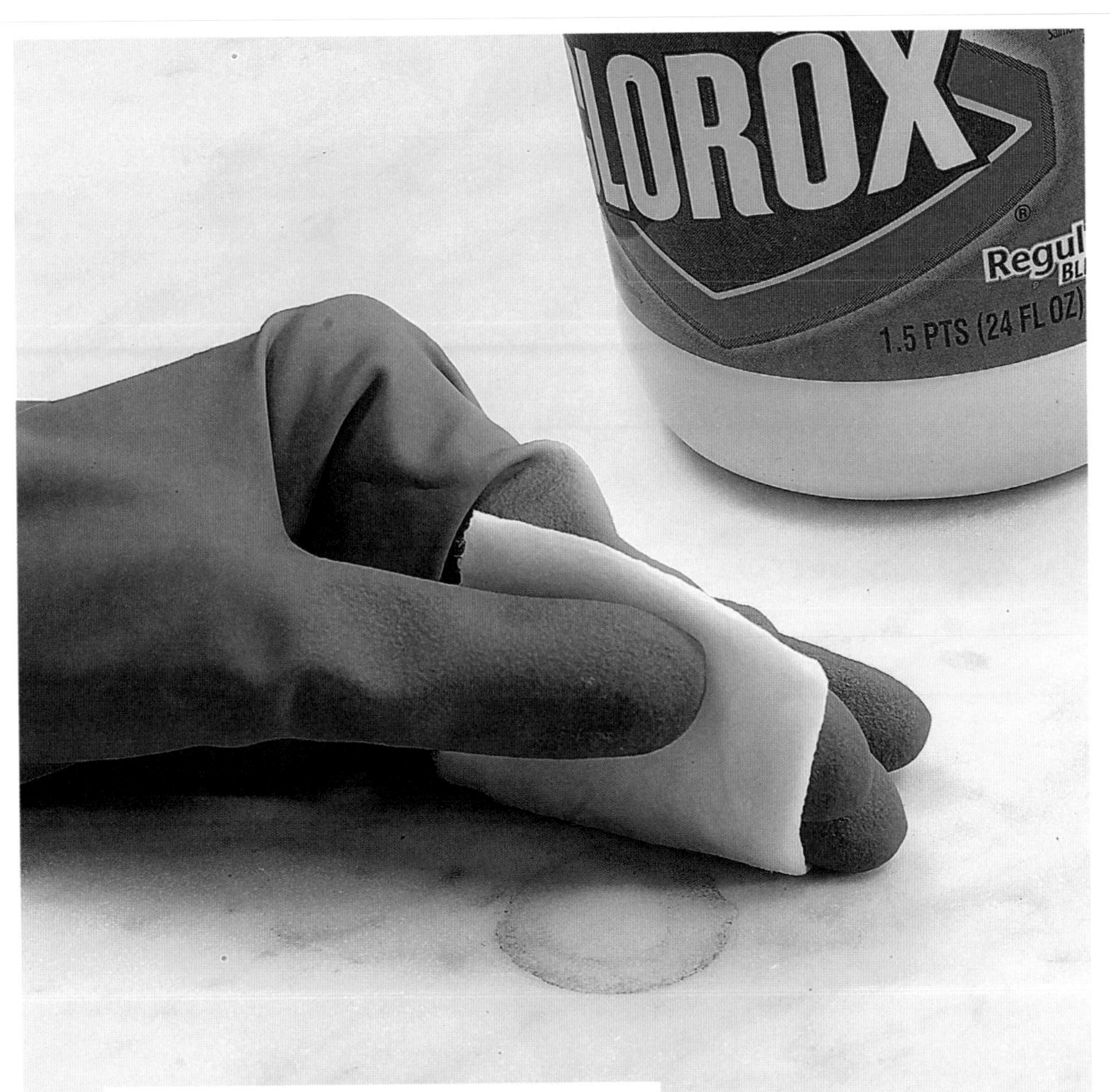


## Bleach Away Stains

Remove stains from marble, cultured marble or plastic laminate with a bleach-soaked paper towel. Lay the towel over the stain, then cover it with a cup to contain the bleach odor and leave it in place overnight. If the stain has faded but not disappeared, just repeat the process. Test this trick in a hidden area first; it could discolor the surface.

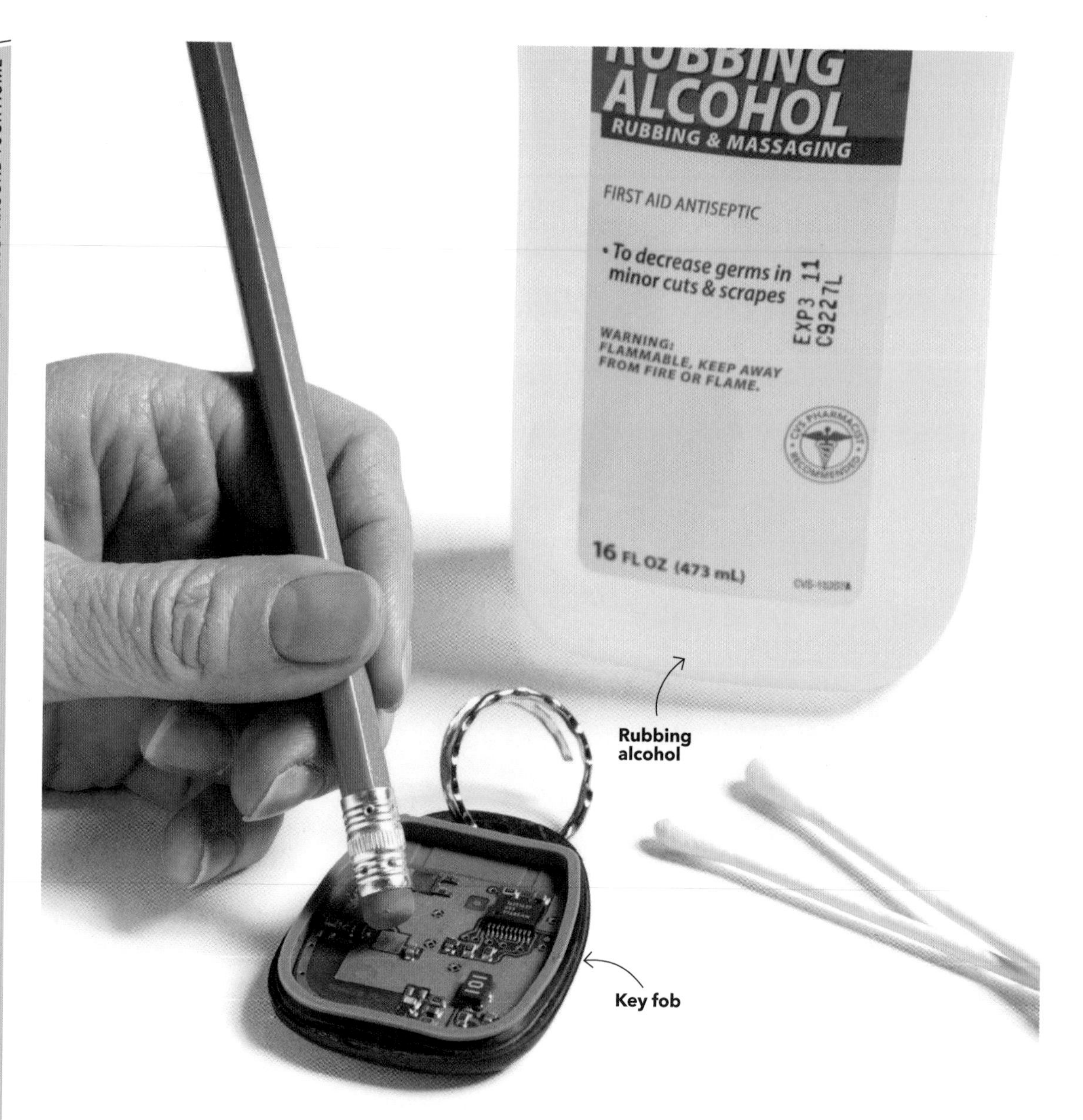


# Quick Key Fob Fix

If your key fob or TV remote stops working, try this fix before shelling out the dough for an expensive replacement. Take the cover off the fob and use a clean pencil eraser to remove the gummy stuff where the buttons touch the circuit board. Then use a cotton swab dipped in rubbing alcohol to clean the same area. Reassemble the fob or remote, and it should work like new!

## DISHWASHER DOUBLE-DUTY

It can take forever to wash greasy dust off hard-to-clean items like switch plates, light fixture covers and stove drip pans. Why not do it the easy way and just throw them into the dishwasher? It really works great on items made of plastic, aluminum or steel—especially items like vent covers that have lots of gaps and detailing. Toss them into the top rack and send them through a normal cycle. Don't do this with things that are enameled, painted, plated, or made of brass or wood.

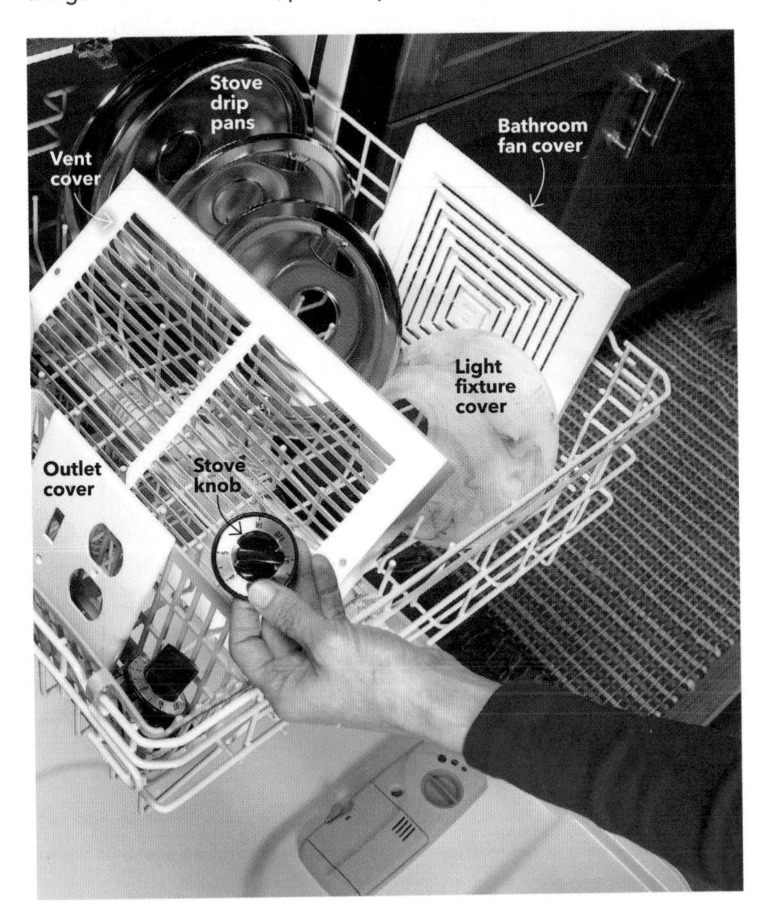

# SPLASH-PROOF WALLS

With muddy dogs, hunters and teenagers coming and going, it can be tough to keep the walls in your back entryway from getting dirty and needing to be repainted all the time. (Maybe that is why it's called a mudroom.) Solve the problem by "wallpapering" the walls with inexpensive vinyl flooring. Now all you have to do is wipe it down for it to look like new again.

## Duster for the Vertically Challenged

Dusting ceiling fans and other high, out-of-reach objects is a real chore. To make it easier, wrap a dryer sheet around a clean paint roller and secure the ends with rubber bands. Attach an extension handle to the roller and dust away.

## Self-Cleaning Barbecue

If you're going to do a self-clean cycle on your oven, do double duty! Grab the grease-covered racks out of your barbecue grill and throw those in too. The self-clean cycle will incinerate stubborn deposits with little to no work on your part.

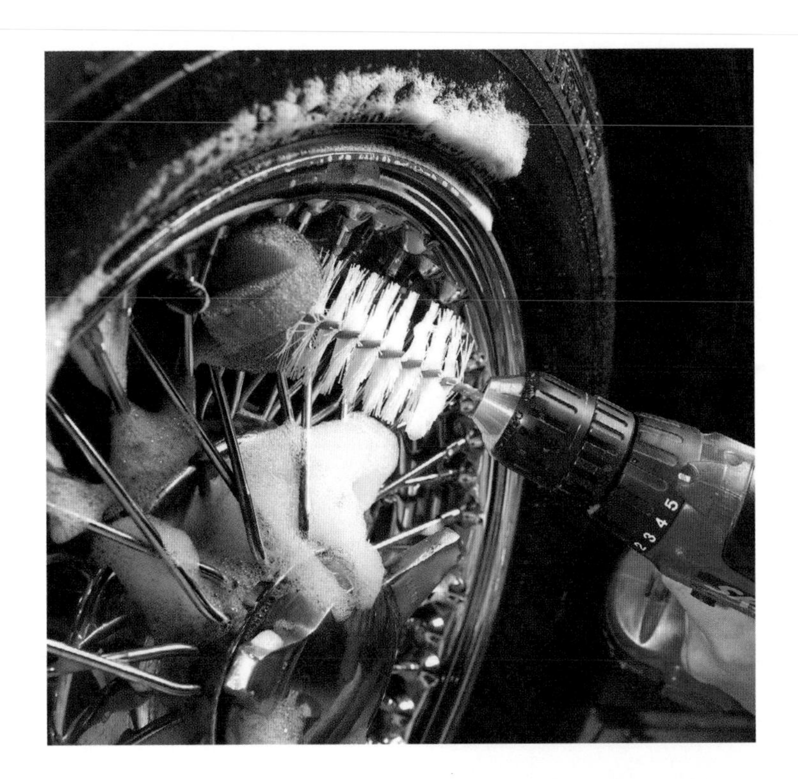

## CORDLESS SCRUBBER FOR TIGHT SPOTS

Clean out tire rims, tiny openings and other hard-to-scrub spots quickly with a bottle brush and a cordless drill. Just cut the handle off the brush, put it in a cordless drill and start scrubbing.

## KEEP KITCHEN CABINETS CLEAN DURING REMODELING

Knocking down old walls or sanding drywall creates a fine dust that coats everything in the house. But you can keep it out of cabinets by sealing them temporarily with a self-sticking plastic wrap (one brand is Glad Press'N Seal).

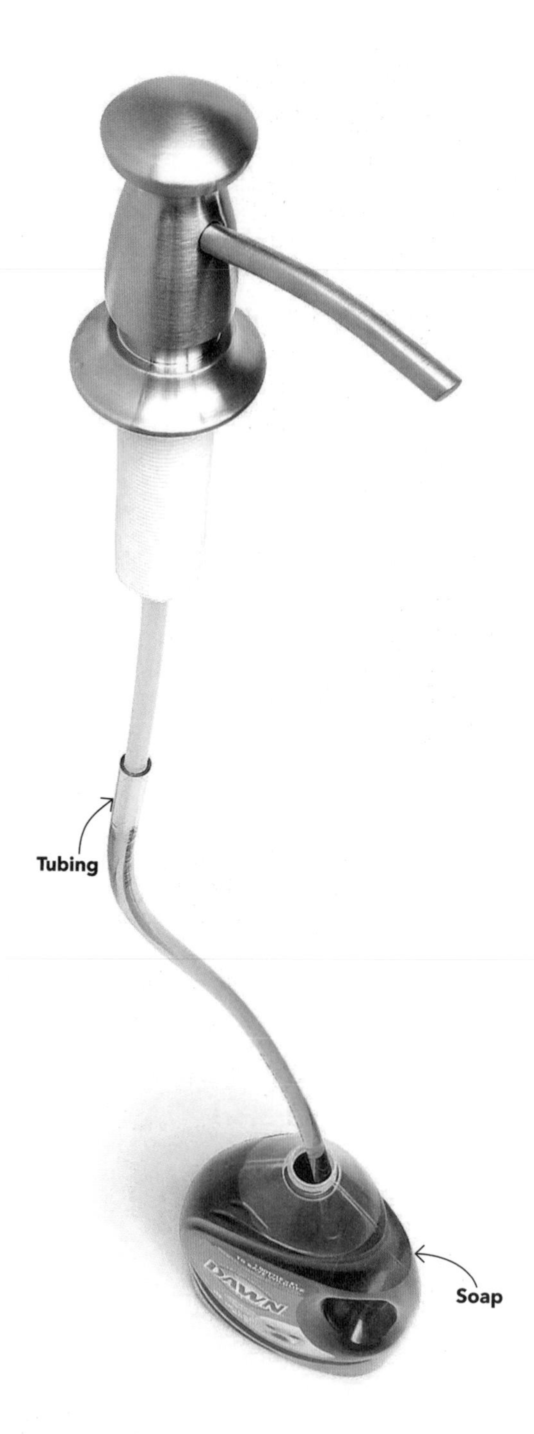


## ENDLESS SOAP DISPENSER

If you have pump soap dispensers built into your sink top, you might find the reservoir so small that you are constantly refilling it. To solve this problem, replace the plastic straw on the pump base with a few feet of plastic tubing, and then buy a large bottle of soap and place it in the cabinet under the sink. Stick the other end of the tubing into the bottle. It'll last for months!

## Vinegar Gets the Gunk

You should keep lawn equipment clean, but for some stuff, that's easier said than done. For items like a string trimmer, scrub off muck with a dish brush and white vinegar. It takes about 15 minutes for a trimmer to go from gunky to great.

# Window-Washing Smarts

When you're up on a ladder washing windows, it can be a hassle to keep all your equipment within easy reach. For more convenience, loop your belt through the handles of two old plastic shopping bags so the bags hang at your sides. Put window spray and a roll of paper towels in one bag and used paper towels in the other. Sure, you might look a little goofy, but it sure beats going up and down the ladder to retrieve a dropped roll of paper towels.

# MAGNET DRAGNET

After you've had remodeling or roofing work done on your home, it's not unusual to get a flat tire from old nails or other hardware left behind. As soon as the roofing contractors' taillights are out of your driveway, rig up this drag using rope and a 24-in. magnetic tool bar. Make sure to drag it everywhere you'll be driving. It picks up much more metal debris than the wheeled type, which doesn't actually touch the ground, and it definitely beats the cost and hassle of a flat tire.

## EASIER CAR CLEANING

Cleaning out a car with a vacuum cleaner can be a lengthy process, and the vacuum doesn't always do a successful job of getting into all the nooks and crannies. Here's a much better solution: Use a leaf blower instead. Open all four doors, take out the floor mats and hit the power switch. The leaf blower cleans faster than a vacuum, and it blows out every speck of dirt and dust.

# Shop Vacuum Prescreen

You can use a shop vacuum for many woodworking chores, including collecting dust from every power tool that features a dust port. But the vacuum's filter quickly plugs with coarse dust from the table saw and the finer dust from sanding. Solve part of the issue by placing window screen over the filter. Now the coarse particles will be filtered out and stay at the bottom of the tank, and the filter won't plug as fast.

# Handy Sanding Disc Cleaner

Sandpaper loses effectiveness when it's clogged with sawdust or pitch. Gum eraser-type sandpaper cleaners work really well, but if you don't have one on hand, the sole of an old sneaker works too. Turn on your sander and then slide the rubber sole along the disc or belt, using just enough pressure to remove the sanding debris.

# Metal Shavings Collector

A simple way to keep metal fragments and shavings from flying all over when you're drilling is to put a magnet next to the bit. This keeps metal bits off the floor, your vise and your body. When you're done, just clean off the magnet over a trash can. Don't forget to wear eye protection (doctor's orders!).

## QUICK SANDING CLEANUP

If you're sanding a small drywall patch or drilling a hole and you don't want to haul out the vacuum cleaner to clean up after such a small job, use a fabric softener sheet instead. It acts like a magnet for sawdust and drywall dust—one or two swipes and your cleanup is done.

# EXTREME CLEANING

## A home improvement with a huge payoff

**YOU PROBABLY DON'T THINK OF** cleaning as home improvement, but a thorough cleaning really is a powerful way to improve your home. Things that look old, worn and in need of replacement sometimes just need a good scrubbing! (Some of us at *Family Handyman* have learned that lesson recently.) Here are a few tips for what—and how—to clean up around your home.

# Focus on the Bathroom

Cleaning the bathroom might take you more time than the rest of the house combined. But it's essential, especially if you're selling. If there's one room potential buyers are extra picky about, it's the bathroom. It should be spotless.

## Glass Shower Doors

Built-up soap scum seems impossible to remove. Pick up polishing compound at a home center or an auto parts store and use it with an auto buffer to polish off the offending scum. If you don't own a buffer, you can buy one for as little as $20 or borrow one from a gearhead friend. If possible, take the doors out to the garage to avoid messing up the bathroom.

## Caulking

Trying to clean caulk often just isn't worth the effort and time. If it's covered with mold or mildew, just cut it out and recaulk.

# Declutter First

Cleaning your house is far easier once you remove clutter, and that's something most of us need to do anyway. If you're selling, don't just put everything in the garage. That's a turnoff for potential buyers. Move your stuff off-site.

**DONATE IT.**
Donating your goods is a nice way to get rid of usable items without the hassle of selling them. It's perfect if you have a lot of stuff and limited time.

**SELL IT.**
If you have time and you'd like to make a little extra cash, sell unwanted things online. Keep in mind that you'll have to check messages and be available for people coming over to buy your stuff. It can be a big hassle.

**PUT IT ON THE CURB.**
Setting free stuff on the curb is probably the quickest and easiest way to get rid of it. People will take anything that's free! The drawback is that if you itemize deductions on your tax returns, you won't get a receipt to count the item as a charitable donation. You can also list free items on Craigslist.com.

**TRASH IT.**
If you have a lot of junk, throwing it all in a dumpster or Bagster bag is an easy and gratifying experience. A small dumpster (about 10 cu. yds.) typically costs about $300.

**STORE IT.**
For the items you're keeping but not using for staging, mobile storage containers are the way to go. Have one dropped at your house, fill it up, and then the company will haul it off to a temporary storage facility or your new home. The cost varies depending on the container size and the distance of the move. A long-distance move runs about $800.

## Tile Grout

Try a bleach pen to take your grout from grungy to great. This method can be pretty tedious, but the payoff is crisp, clean grout lines. Use the pen to "draw" bleach across the grout lines. The pen allows you to target the grout without getting bleach all over the tile. Wait 10 minutes and then rinse.

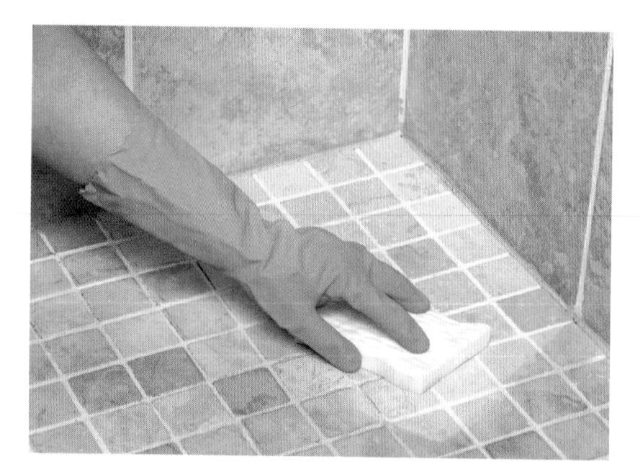

## Tile

Magic Eraser sponges (or other brands) make short work of cleaning tile. It's easy–dampen the sponge and rub it on the offending mess. In most cases, the mess will come right off. These sponges are especially useful for removing ground-in dirt from porous floor tile and cleaning those pesky nonslip strips in the bottom of your tub.

## Rust Stains

To clean rust from toilets and other porcelain surfaces, add three parts water to one part rust remover (Acid Magic is one brand we like). Use a sprayer, brush or foam pad to apply the mixture to the rust stains, then watch them dissolve. Rinse with clear water. You can also use the acid full strength for stubborn stains. Avoid getting it on metal parts because they can discolor. Acid Magic is available online and at hardware stores.

### Faucets and Fixtures

Scrub faucets and fixtures with a calcium, lime and rust remover, such as CLR, and an old toothbrush.

### Exhaust Fan

Turn on the fan and blast out the dust with canned air. The fan will blow the dust outside. This works on the return air grilles of your central heating /cooling system too. Run the system so the return airflow will carry the dust to the filter. You'll find canned air at home centers, usually in the electrical supplies aisle.

## Dig into the Details

Some cleaning jobs get overlooked, either because we're so used to these areas not being clean or because we just don't like doing them. Pay attention to the following:

- Ceiling fan blades
- Light fixtures
- Baseboards/trim/ door frames
- Handrails
- Furniture feet
- Fingerprints
- Furnace and water heater exteriors
- Exposed pipes and ductwork
- Washer and dryer
- Inside cabinets and drawers
- Walls and ceilings
- Curtains
- Underneath appliances
- Trash cans
- Doorknobs
- Dishwasher
- Throw pillows

#### WINDOWS

Your windows present the view as well as let in natural light. You can hire a window cleaning service, but if you'd like to do it yourself, go to familyhandyman.com and search for "how to clean windows."

#### CARPET

If the carpet is reasonably clean, don't go beyond vacuuming it. Carpet is the last thing buyers look at and doesn't give a big return on investment. If there's hardwood underneath, consider removing the carpet.

#### GET A CLEANING SERVICE

You can hire a pro to do a deep cleaning. At about $500 for a 1,400-sq.-ft. home, it's definitely worth considering. Check off a weekend's worth of drudgery by writing a check!

#### DON'T CLEAN; REPLACE

Some things just aren't worth the effort to clean. You'll save time and money and get better results by simply replacing the following items with new:

- Shower curtains
- Switch plates
- Mini blinds
- Showerheads

# CHAPTER 2

# ORGANIZATION

PING

# SLICK CHARGER ID TAGS

Electrical drawers always get clogged with chargers and transformers from various cameras, phones and who knows what else. They look alike, so it's hard to find the one you need in the tangled mess. Try this: Label each one as soon as you get it. Then you'll find it instantly.

## PVC Curling Iron Holsters

Curling irons kept on counters or toilet tanks get in the way, and the cords are always falling into the sink or onto the floor. Solve the problem with PVC pipe. Use hook-and-loop tape to attach 5-in. lengths of 2-in.-diameter pipe to the vanity door to hold your curling irons (or measure your curling irons to see how long your "holsters" need to be). Do the same thing with 3-in. pieces of 1-1/2-in.-diameter pipe to hold the cords. Let your curling irons cool before you stow them away.

# Towel Bar for Appliances

Some dishwashers don't have a handle you can use as a towel bar, but you can add a magnetic curtain rod designed for steel entry doors. Many stainless steel appliances won't hold magnets, but some newer ones will.

## DISAPPEARING REMOTES

If your remote controls are cluttering your coffee table and getting lost behind sofa cushions, here's how to tidy up: Apply adhesive-backed hook-and-loop strips to the underside of the coffee table and to the backs of the remotes. To avoid snags on upholstery and clothing, put the soft (loop) material on the remotes. Now all the controls will be hidden from view, but you'll always know where to find them. Hook-and-loop strips are available at home centers and discount and hardware stores.

# BRILLIANT BUNGEE CORD STORAGE

Bungee cords always seem to end up in a tangled mess. To keep them organized, screw a scrap piece of closet shelving to the wall and hook the cords along its length. Now it'll be easy to find the one you need.

## Portable Clothes Pods

Here's a cool way to pack your clothes for moving. First, cut a hole in the center of the bottom of a large trash bag. Grab a handful of clothes by the hanger hooks and slip the bag over the clothes, pulling the hooks through the hole. Use a zip tie or wire to hold the hooks together, and then tie the bag's open end shut. Your clothes stay clean in these easily portable pods, and you never have to take them off the hangers!

## Key Identifier

If you have trouble telling a few similar-looking keys apart, try this easy fix. Take a file and cut notches in the sides of a couple of keys. Even in the dark you'll know which key is which just by feeling them.

# CLOTHESPIN HAMPER

Someday your old cloth clothespin hamper will fall apart, and an empty plastic plant hanger basket could be a wonderful replacement. Just give it a thorough cleaning and drill a couple of extra 1/4-in. drainage holes into the bottom. The plastic hook can slide easily along the line, and the basket has more than enough room for clothespins.

# GARDENING AND WORK GLOVES HANG-UP

Losing gardening and work gloves in the shed is worse than losing socks in the dryer. You'd be lucky to find one glove on the floor and the other one stuck in an empty flowerpot. To stop losing gloves and to organize them, hang binder clips on nails. Your gloves will always be dry and together in a matched set.

# HANDY BENCH AND TOOL BUCKET

A 5-gallon bucket comes in handy out in the garden—and not just for collecting weeds. You can load it with all your gardening tools and carry them easily from place to place. If it starts to rain, protect your tools with the lid. But here's the best part: It doubles as a portable stool when you need to rest or do some pruning. The only problem is that the lid can be hard to pry off. Solve that by cutting off all but two of the plastic tabs. The lid will go on and off in a snap.

## Clear Leaf Bags for Storage

Clear leaf bags aren't only good for collecting leaves. Because they're large, you can cover lawn chairs, cushions, space heaters, fans and other items to keep them dust-free in the rafters or on shelving in the garage. The best part is that you can easily find items at a glance because the bags are transparent—a feature old black garbage bags lack!

# Garden Tool Nook

Here's a classic hint that puts an old mailbox to work and really brightens up a garden. Screw the mailbox to a post and sink the post in the garden. It's a perfect place to store gardening gloves and small tools. If you're feeling artistic, paint something clever on the mailbox. What a charming way to add a convenient storage nook outside!

## GARDEN/GARAGE TOOL CADDY

Wood and plastic lattice are good for more than building fences—they can make a fantastic caddy to organize garden shovels, hoes and brooms. You can even install casters so the contraption will scoot easily into a corner of the garage. Works great!

## LAWN CHEMICAL INVENTORY

It's easy to buy duplicate fungicides and weed killers if you don't know what you have. Not only that, but you can eventually amass too many to remember how they're used (and reading the small print on the labels is no fun). So put all your lawn chemicals into a plastic bin, make a simple spreadsheet on the computer and attach it to the front of the bin. Now you can easily see what you have and how to use it.

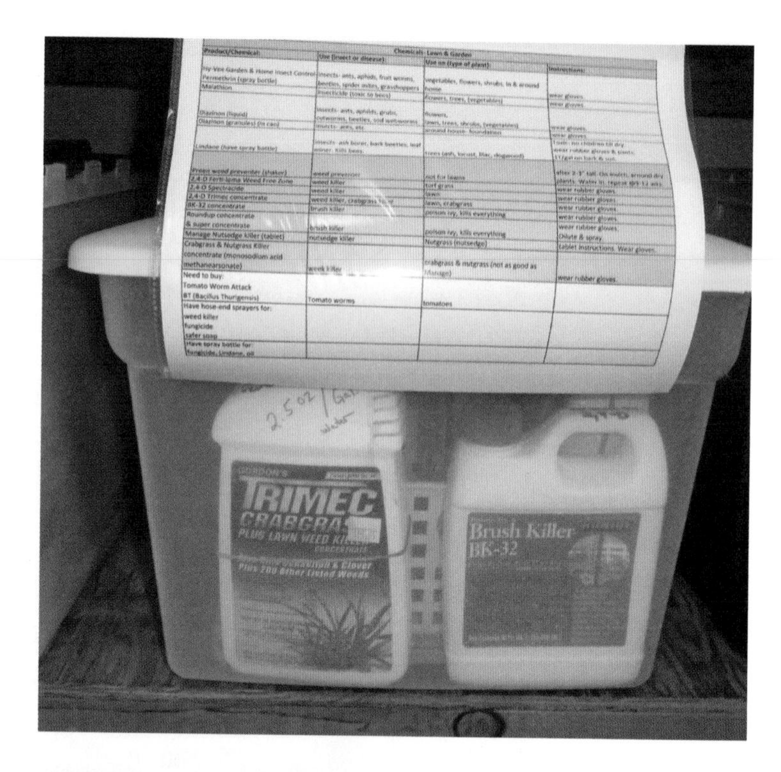

## TANGLE-FREE JUMPER CABLE STORAGE

In cold climates, having jumper cables at the ready is serious business—but for some reason they always seem to reside under seats or tangled up in a heap beneath some other stuff in the trunk. For a better storage option, keep them coiled around a spare tire under the false floor of your trunk. Now you'll always know where they are and they'll never get tangled.

## Movable Bike Rack

Tired of that bike hanging in your way? Build this movable bike rack from a 2x4 and a pair of bicycle hooks. Cut four 3-1/2-in. blocks, stack them in twos and screw them together. Now screw one stack on the end of a 4-ft. 2x4 and repeat the process on the other end. Drill a hole in the middle of each stack and screw in the bicycle hooks. Lay the rack across your garage ceiling joists, and hang your bike from the hooks. When you need to get behind the bike, simply slide the entire rack out of the way.

## Useful T-Rack Storage

Here's a hanging T-rack that combines two different types of storage space—one side is a typical U-shaped rack for storing pipe and other items that might roll off, the other side is a horizontal rack that allows you to load and unload lumber and molding from the side instead of from the ends. This is useful in garages and basements where space is tight.

# FISHING ROD ORGANIZER

All you need to keep your fishing rods tangle-free is a length of 3-in.-diameter PVC pipe and a foam swimming pool noodle. Drill 1-in. holes in the PVC pipe spaced every 4 in. Use a utility knife to cut slits in the foam noodle, spacing them 4 in. apart also. Line up the pool noodle on the wall so that at least two of the slits sit over studs. Pull those slits apart, slide in a fender washer and screw the noodle to the wall with 2-in. screws. Then screw the PVC pipe to the wall beneath the pool noodle at a comfortable height and insert your fishing rods.

## BBQ TOOL ORGANIZER

Tired of all your cooking tools taking up valuable space on your grill's side tray? Here's the perfect solution: Screw hooks to the underside of your deck railing. Now you can hang each tool on its own hook. It's a great way to keep your tools out of the way yet right where you need them.

# Overhead Storage Space

The space between the floor joists in an unfinished basement is a perfect spot to store leftover trim and boards. Buy some chain, S-hooks and eye screws to make some corrals to hold the items in place. It's easy now to see your inventory and slip a piece out, or to remove the chain and sort through the entire bundle.

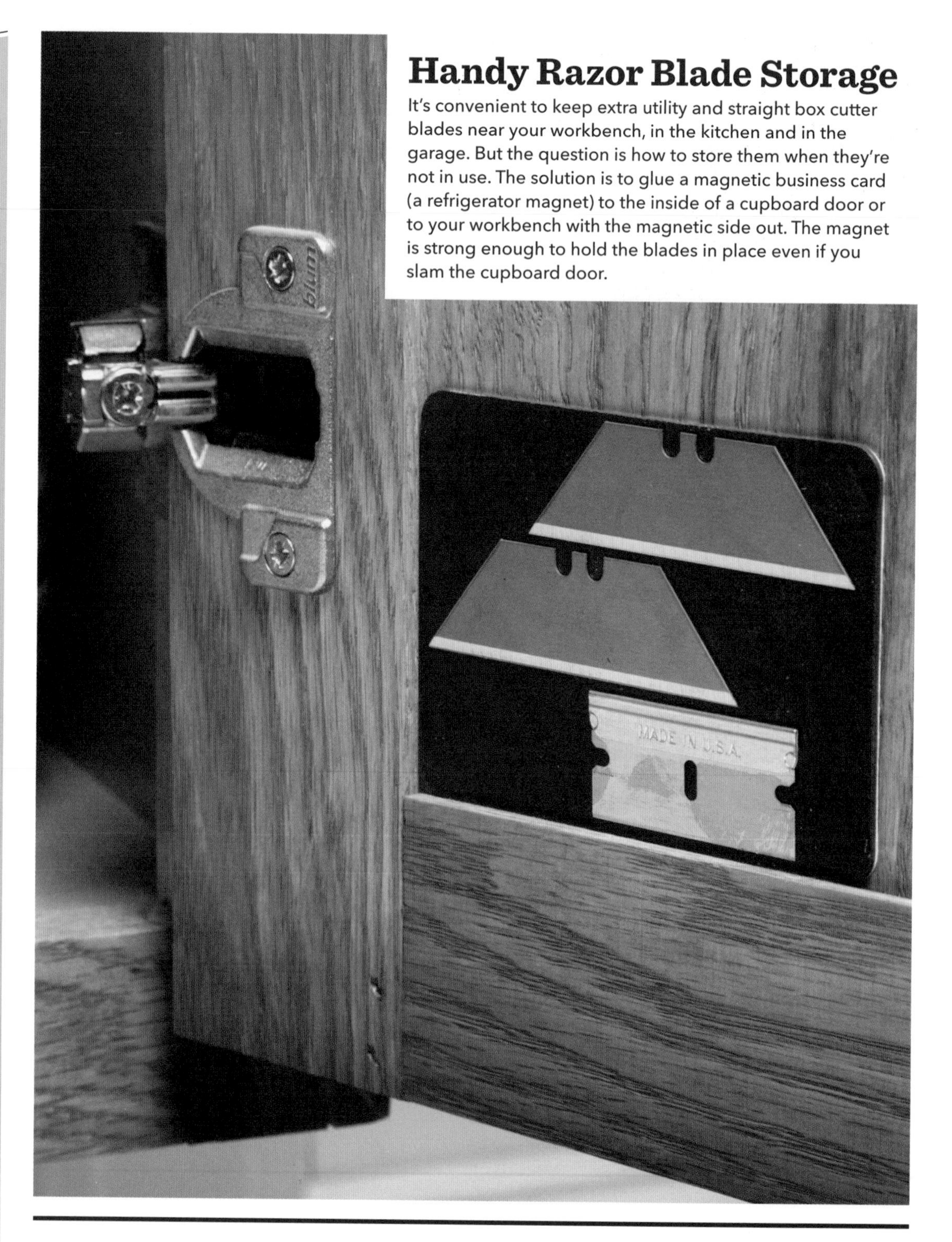


# Handy Razor Blade Storage

It's convenient to keep extra utility and straight box cutter blades near your workbench, in the kitchen and in the garage. But the question is how to store them when they're not in use. The solution is to glue a magnetic business card (a refrigerator magnet) to the inside of a cupboard door or to your workbench with the magnetic side out. The magnet is strong enough to hold the blades in place even if you slam the cupboard door.

## TIDIER TOOL TRAYS

A piece of short-pile carpet on the bottom of each tray in your tool chest will keep tools from shifting and knocking about. The next time you open the tray, the tools will still be laid out nice and neat, just the way you left them. Another benefit: less noise.

## NO-TANGLE RATCHET STRAPS

Ratchet straps must have a self-tangling feature—they're always twisted when you want to use them. Bundling them with rubber bands is one option, but the bands break as they get old. Instead, pick up a roll of stretch wrap and put it in a canvas bag with your ratchet straps. When you're done using a strap, bundle it and wrap it tight with a few rounds of stretch wrap. You can fold back the end portion so it's easy to unwrap the next time. Now your straps are always ready to use.

## SCREWDRIVER ORGANIZER

Here's an easy way to store screwdrivers for quick access and identification. Drill holes through a length of PVC pipe, screw it to the wall, and organize your screwdrivers by type and by size.

# Cool Hardware Organizer

Whether you're taking something apart for repair or getting ready to assemble some flat-pack furniture, having all the hardware organized and not rolling around on your workbench is super helpful. Keep a couple of ice cube trays around your workshop for this purpose.

# Picture-Perfect Tool Wall

If you're moving or remodeling, it can be tricky to put your workshop back together from memory. Photograph your tool wall so that when you land in a new place (or the remodel is done), you can quickly set up your shop wall and place all your tools in exactly the right spot.

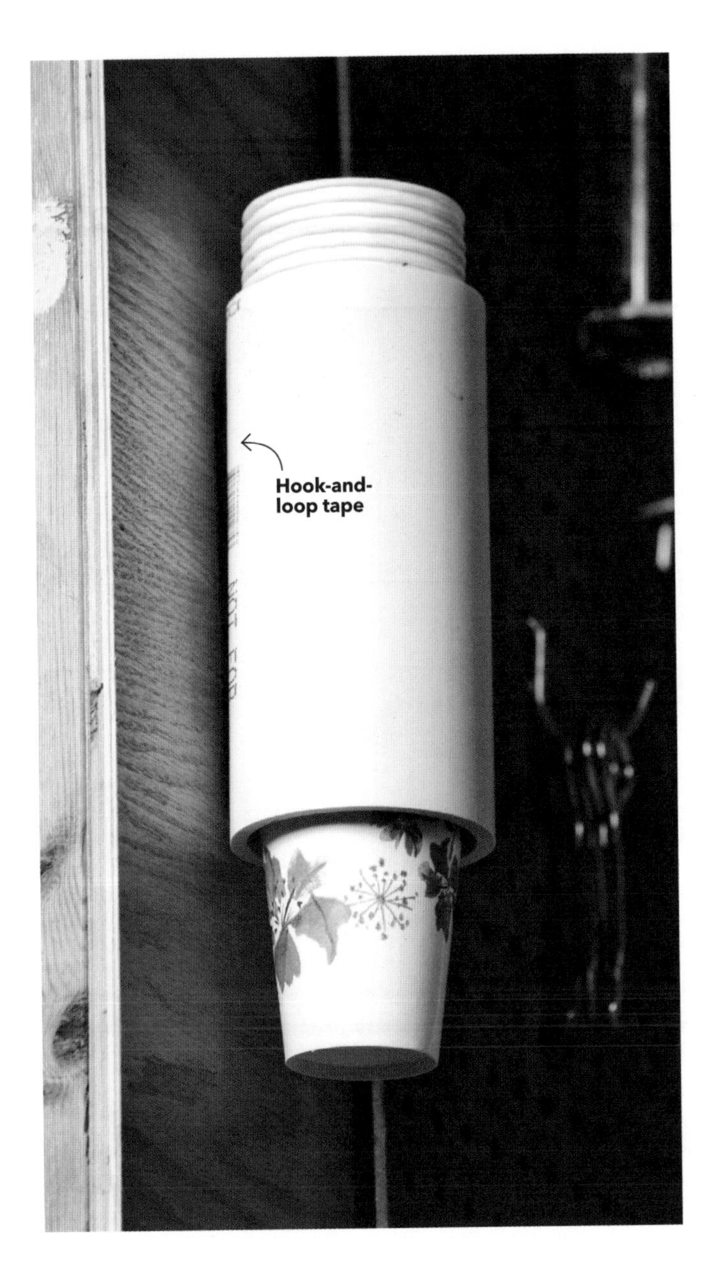


## SHOP CUP DISPENSER

Small paper cups are handy in the shop for holding or mixing small amounts of wood glue, two-part epoxy, spray paint and the like. This simple homemade paper cup dispenser works wonderfully. Measure the diameter of the cups and attach a short length of the same diameter PVC pipe to your wall with hook-and-loop tape. If the cups sit too loosely in the dispenser, just add a bead of silicone inside the bottom lip to keep them tight.

# SAVING HARDWOOD SCRAPS

Short scraps of hardwood are too good to throw away but are hard to store neatly. Buy a 4-ft. tube form made for concrete footings, cut it in half (the cardboard-like material cuts easily) and set the tubes on end. Tack the tubes to a wall or a bench leg so they don't fall over. With wood scraps stored upright, it's easy to find a piece just the right length. Tube forms are available in various diameters at home centers.

## Tool Belt Hardware Organizer

While you're working on projects, your tool belt fills up with random screws, washers, nails, and other odds and ends. And when you want to find something in your belt, you have to take off your gloves and rummage around in all that mess. Here's a simple, helpful time-saver: Toss a magnet into your tool belt. Every small fastener will stick to the magnet. Then all you need to do is grab it and pick off whatever you need. You don't even have to take off your gloves. Awesome!

PING

# THROW & GO BINS

**SHELVES AND CABINETS** are ideal places to store kid stuff, but when you're in a hurry (and kids always are), it is nice to just throw and go. That's why we built these bins. They are great for sports gear but can handle all kinds of random garage clutter.

We wanted something with a little character, so we based our design on a row of old bins at a country store. It was worth the little bit of extra effort to build something that brings back good memories yet serves a practical purpose in the present. These bins have worked so well that we are thinking about building a set for gardening supplies, too.

### CUT THE PARTS

Cut the sides, top and bottom from 3/4-in. plywood using a table saw or circular saw. We used "BC" plywood, which is good enough for paint, but you may want to buy birch veneer plywood if you plan to use stain. This project requires a full sheet of plywood plus a 2 x 4-ft. section. Many home centers carry 4 x 4 ft., and some even stock 2 x 4 ft., so you don't have to buy two full sheets–however, they charge a premium for smaller sheets, and you won't save more than a few bucks. We bought two full sheets and used the leftovers on other projects. The same goes for the 1/4-in. plywood–you need only a 4 x 4-ft. sheet, but a 4 x 8 ft. is a better value.

The fronts of the bins will get the most abuse, so we built them from a solid 1x6 pine board. Solid wood holds up far better than a plywood edge. You can rip down the two center boards when you're cutting up the other parts, but hold off on cutting them to length until the top and bottom boards are in place. That way you can cut them exactly to size.

### MARK THE SIDE PROFILE

This part of the process seems a little tricky, but it's really quite simple if you follow these directions. Hook a tape measure on the bottom front of one of the side boards. Measure up and mark the edge of the board at 0, 4 in., 15-1/2 in., 19-1/2 in., 31 in. and 35 in. Now go back and measure over 4 in. at the following locations: the bottom, 15-1/2 in.,

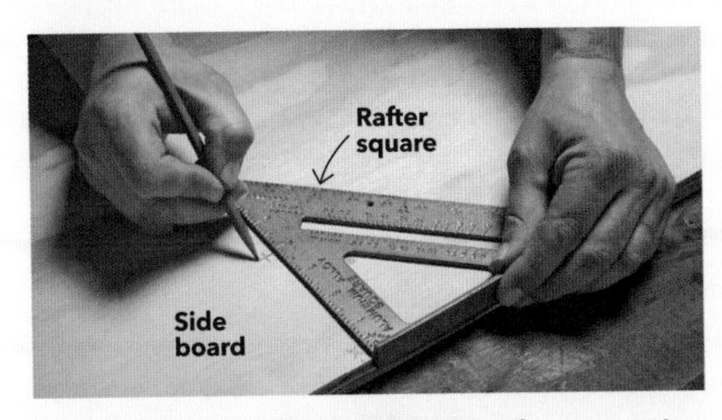


**1 LAY OUT THE SIDE PROFILES.** After measuring and marking the locations of the bin fronts, use a square to mark the recessed portions of front.

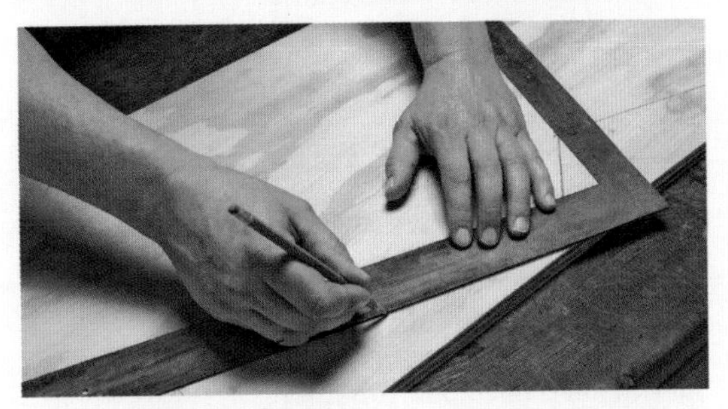

**2 CONNECT THE DOTS.** Use a straightedge to connect the dots. You need to lay out only one side board. Once it's cut, that board will act as a pattern for the rest.

**3 CUT TWO AT A TIME.** Clamp two sides down and cut them both at the same time. That way, if you make any small cutting errors, the pair of sides will still match up. Make most of the cut with a circular saw, and then finish it off with a jigsaw.

31 in. and the top **(Photo 1)**. These marks represent the indented portions of the side. Starting at the end, connect the dots **(Photo 2)**. It's that easy.

### CUT AND SAND THE SIDES

Clamp two side boards down to your work surface. Arrange them so the best sides of the plywood will be on the outside of the bins. Use a circular saw to make most of each cut. (Sometimes it's necessary to hold the blade guard up when you start a cut at an angle.) Finish the cuts with a jigsaw **(Photo 3)**. A handsaw will work fine if you don't own a jigsaw. Sand the edges with 80-grit sandpaper while the sides are still clamped together **(Photo 4)**. Use one of the two cut side boards to mark one of the other uncut side boards, and repeat the process.

If you have already chosen a color for your project, now would be a good time to sand and finish all the parts. That way, you'll have to only touch up the fastener holes after assembly. Some of the plywood edges may have voids, and they can easily be filled with some wood putty or patching compound.

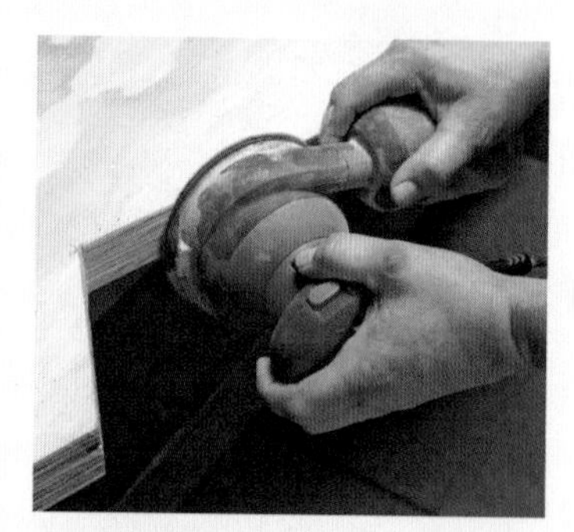

**4 SAND TWO AT A TIME.** Smooth out the cuts before you unclamp the sides. Make sure to keep each pair together when you assemble the bins.

**5 ASSEMBLE THE BINS.** Build the bin sections before you install the top and the bottom. If you have a brad nailer, make assembly easier by tacking all the parts together before you drive in the screws.

### ASSEMBLE THE BINS

Lay out two of the sides back to back with the good sides of the plywood facing down. Using a straightedge, mark lines in between the notches to serve as reference lines for the bottoms of the bins. The bottom of the unit will serve as the bottom of the lowest bins, so fasten the bottom on the second lowest bin first. Align the board above the reference line.

Fasten each bottom and front with three 1-1/2-in. brads. Once it's put together, go back and reinforce it all with two 2-in. trim-head screws in each side of every board.

Once the bottoms are in place, come back and install the 1x6 fronts **(Photo 5)**. Align them flush with the outside edge of the plywood. You'll notice a small gap between the bin bottom and the front. This makes assembly easier, especially if your side cuts weren't perfect. It won't be noticeable when it's up against the wall. Once the first bank of bins is done, assemble the second one.

### FINISH IT UP

Fasten the top and bottom flush with the outside edges of the bins. Again, drive three brads into each side board and then go back and secure them with a couple of trim-head screws.

Use the 1/4-in. plywood back to square up the project. Start with the two factory-cut sides of the plywood. Start fastening it to the top or bottom, making sure it's perfectly flush with the edge. Then fasten one side, working away from the fastened top or bottom, straightening and nailing as you go. Install one screw through the back into each bin bottom for extra support. Before you finish the other two sides, set up the project and check that things are square.

Measure between the two banks of bins, and cut your center boards to that size. Pin them in with brads and secure them with a screw. The center boards can be located anywhere you want depending on the type of items you're going to store. If your project will sit on concrete, you may want to install strips of treated lumber on the bottom. Rip 5/8-in. strips of treated lumber and tack them onto the perimeter of the bottom.

You can screw the project to the wall if you know your kids will be using it as a ladder. All that's left is to go tell the family that there are no more excuses for throwing stuff on the floor.

**FIGURE A**
**BIN OVERVIEW**

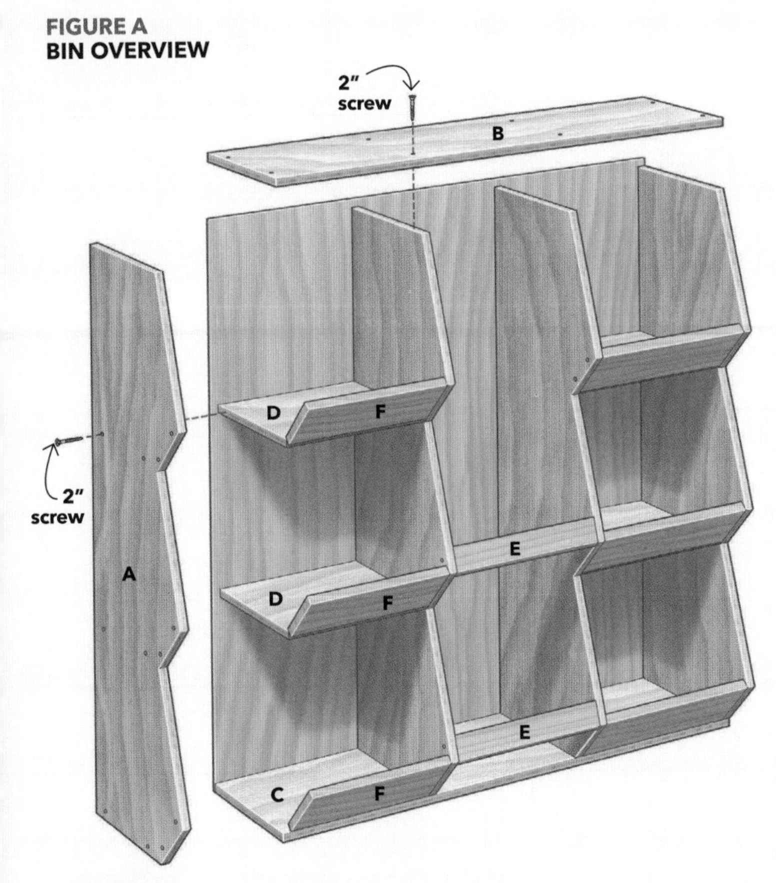


**FIGURE B**
**SIDE LAYOUT**

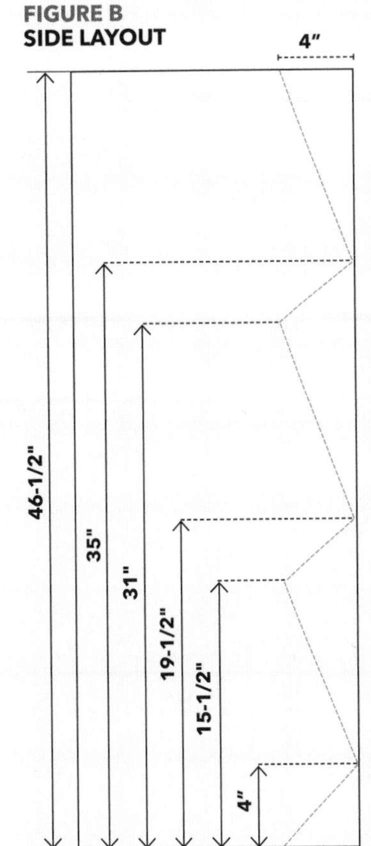


**FIGURE C**
**CUTTING DIAGRAM FOR 3/4" PLYWOOD**

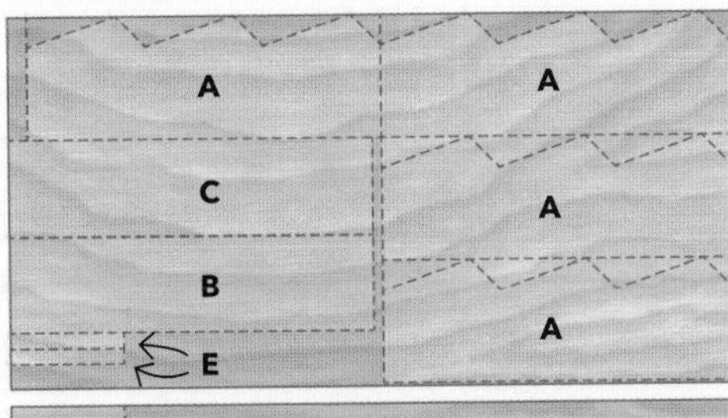

## CUTTING LIST

| KEY | QTY. | SIZE & DESCRIPTION |
|---|---|---|
| A | 4 | 15-7/8" x 46-1/2" x 3/4" BC sanded plywood (sides) |
| B | 1 | 12-1/2" x 48" x 3/4" BC sanded plywood (top) |
| C | 1 | 12-1/2" x 48" x 3/4" BC sanded plywood (bottom) |
| D | 4 | 15" x 11-1/4" x 3/4" BC sanded plywood (bin bottom) |
| E | 2 | 2" x approx. 15" BC sanded plywood (center board) |
| F | 6 | 15" x 5-1/2" pine 1x6 (bin front) |

## MATERIALS LIST

| ITEM | QTY. |
|---|---|
| 4' x 8' x 3/4" BC sanded plywood | 2 |
| 1x6 x 8' pine | 1 |
| 4' x 8' x 1/4" underlayment plywood | 1 |
| 2" trim-head screws | |
| 1-1/2" 18-gauge brads | |
| Gallon of paint/primer | |

# CHAPTER 3

# MAINTENANCE

TRACTION
SAND WILL NOT FREEZE

## Easy-to-Read Circuit Breakers

Switching off circuit breakers in the basement can be tricky; you might not be able to see the stamped numbers on the electrical panel because it's dark. There's no need to squint–just make them easier to see with a little bit of white painter's caulk. Put a dab on each of the numbers and wipe off the excess with your finger so you'll have easy-to-read numbers.

# SLAM BEGONE

Heavy, solid-core interior doors are often quite noisy when slammed shut. To cut down on the ruckus, stick small pieces of foam weather stripping on the door side of the jamb's stop. If the door won't close all the way after installing the weather stripping, you might need to adjust the position of the jamb's strike plate. There are a few different thicknesses at the home center, so try to figure out the ideal thickness before you shop.

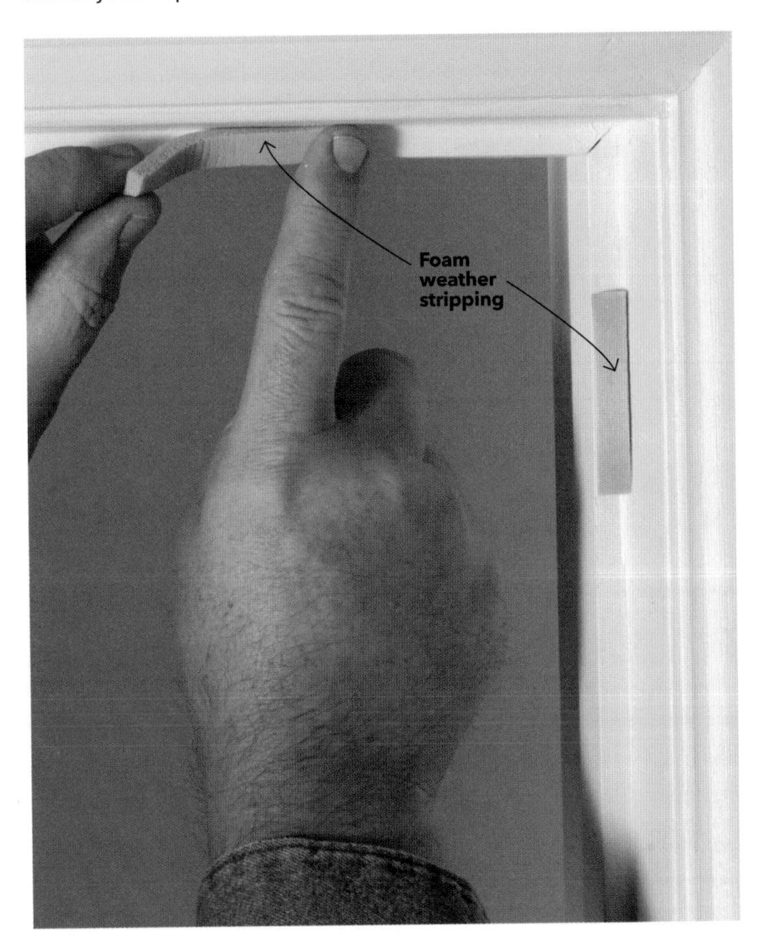

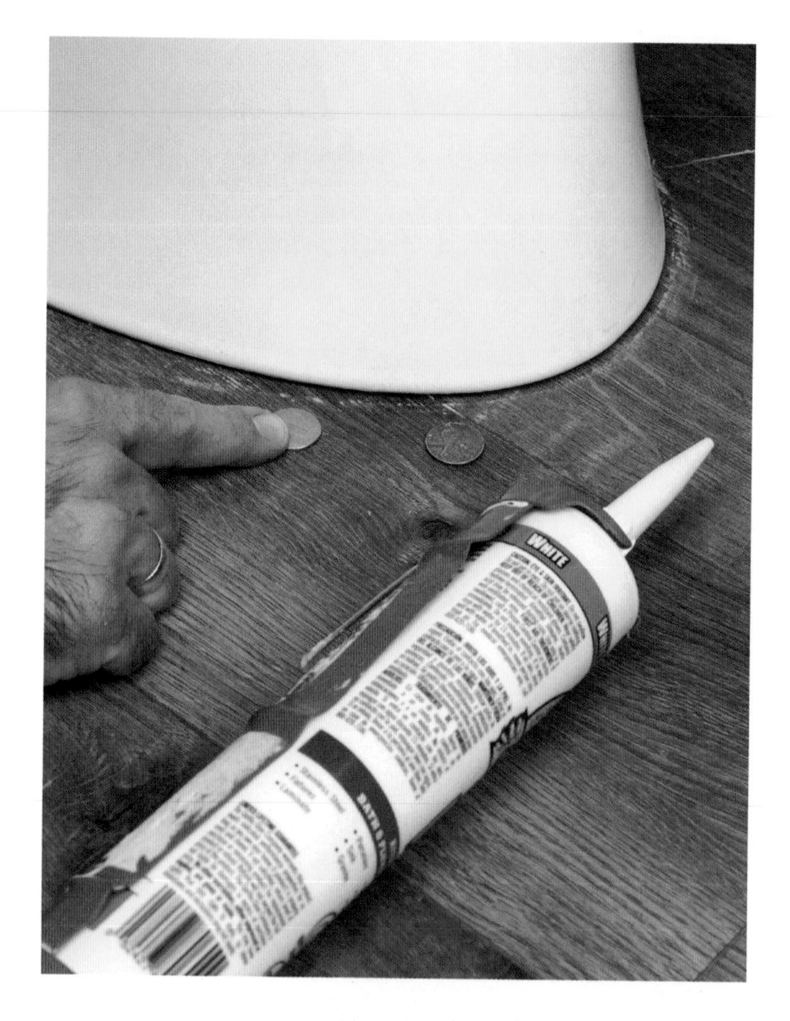


## A PENNY FOR YOUR TOILET SHIMS

You can use spare change as shims to level a toilet. Coins provide a firm seat, and each denomination is a different thickness. Simply slide as many coins as necessary under the toilet until it's completely level. Then tighten the flange bolts, and caulk along the floor as usual. The caulk will hide the coins. Washers work well too.

# Scratch-Free Showerheads

Don't learn the hard way that pliers can scratch a new showerhead. Whenever you need to replace one, wrap some duct tape around the jaws of your pliers to offer protection for the chrome finish.

# Fix for Your Noisy Floors

Here's a super-simple fix for squeaking floor joists: Screw a 1-1/2-in. corner bracket to the joist about 1/8 in. below the subfloor. Then when you drive a screw up into the subfloor, it's pulled tight against the joist. Presto! No more squeak.

# HANDSOME SLIDING DOOR SECURITY

Like a lot of folks, you may need something to secure your sliding patio door. If you are looking for something more stylish than a 2x4 or a metal bar, pick up an oak handrail, then stain and seal it. You can even finish it with an attractive drawer pull. It will work perfectly, is very easy to handle and, best of all, will get tons of compliments.

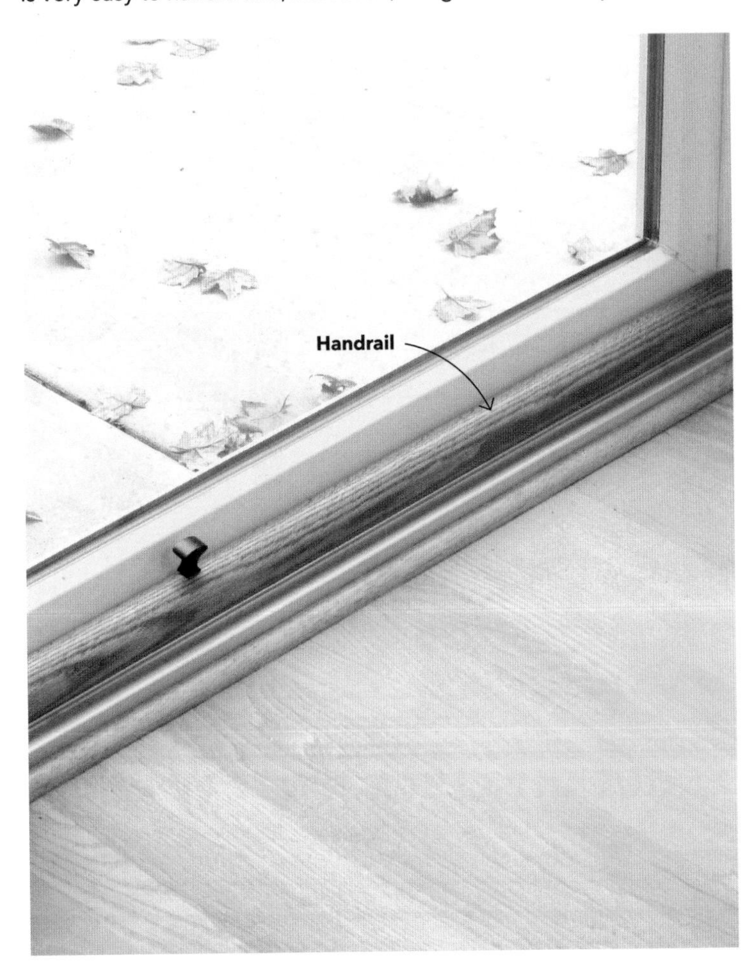

## A SQUEAKY-CLEAN HINGE FIX

You can remedy a squeaky door hinge with a shot of dry lubricant, but protect the surrounding woodwork from overspray by first slitting a piece of thin cardboard and slipping it around the hinge barrel. Wipe away any excess lube to prevent drips, then open and close the door a few times to work the lube into the hinge pin before drying.

# Creaky Chair Tourniquet

Conversation is encouraged around the dining table—unless your chairs are also chiming in. Regluing the joints to tighten things is an option, but what can you do if you don't have strap clamps long enough to wrap around the legs while the glue sets? Wrap thin rope around the chair, tie the end to a stick and twist the stick until the rope is tight. Then tape the stick in place and let the glue dry overnight.

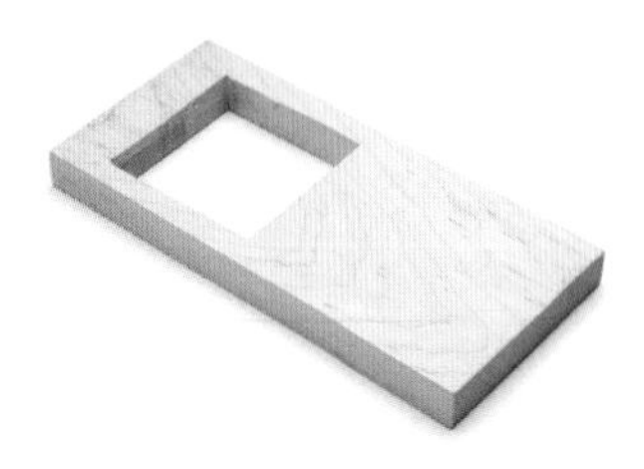

## Stay-Put Sofa

Don't deal with scuffed paint because of your sofa. Fix the problem by making wooden "shoes" for the back two sofa legs. Cut a scrap 1x4 into two short sections and then cut holes to fit the legs. The "shoes" will keep your sofa in its place. If your sofa doesn't have a skirt to hide the shoes, you could stain them to blend in better with your flooring.

## Simple Carpet Protectors

Heavy furniture, such as filing cabinets and grandfather clocks, can leave dents in carpet. To solve that problem, cut leftover carpeting into squares the same size as the furniture. Place the squares on top of the carpet and put the furniture on top of them. The carpet squares blend in with the carpet and keep the wall-to-wall carpet dent free.

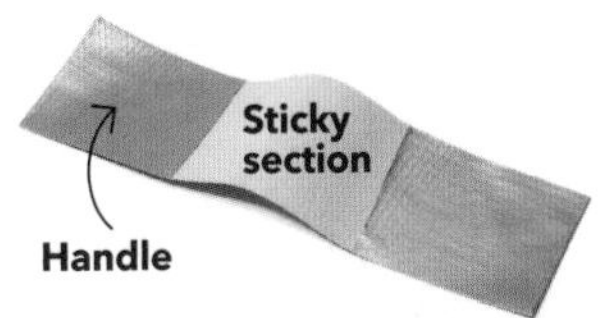


# HOW MANY PIECES OF DUCT TAPE...

...does it take to change a lightbulb? One, if you fold it right. If you've ever tried to unscrew a lightbulb from a recessed fixture, you know how tough it is to get your fingers around it. Use duct tape to make a lightbulb "handle." Rip a piece of duct tape off the roll and fold the ends back over themselves, leaving a sticky section in the middle. Put the sticky section on the bulb, grasp the ends and give the tape a twist. This trick works great—and that's no joke!

# "Hot" Vinyl Tile Removal Tip

Here's a hot tip for removing a damaged vinyl tile that needs replacement. Put a cloth down on the tile, and hold an iron set to medium-high on the cloth for 10 seconds. The cloth keeps the tile from melting but makes it pliable and softens the adhesive backing. Tease a corner free with the tip of a utility knife; the tile will peel right up. This works with both peel-and-stick and glue-down tiles.

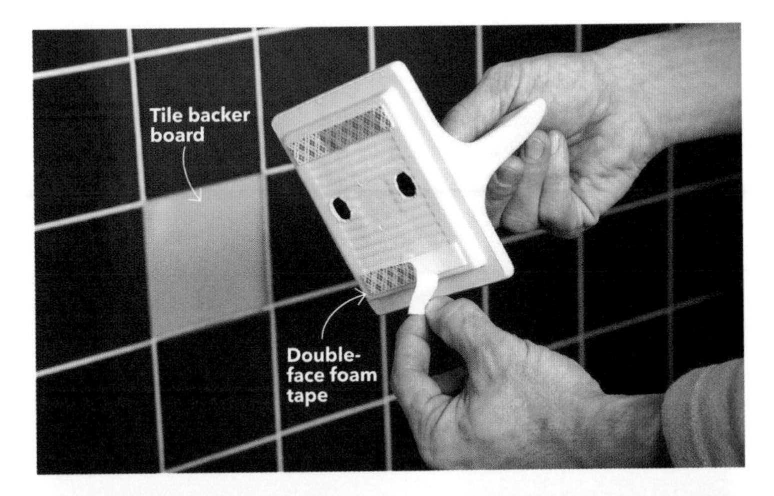

## STAY-PUT SOAP DISH

When installing a ceramic soap dish on a tiled wall, put a couple of strips of double-face foam tape on the back of the soap dish. Align the dish and press it against the tile backer board. Then apply silicone caulk around the edges. The foam tape will hold the dish in place until the caulk cures. This works better than putting tape across the front and prevents the dish from sagging.

# FIRST AID KIT FOR YOUR HOUSE

When making minor household repairs, finding the supplies you need can take longer than the repair itself. Put the items you use most in a plastic container that you can easily carry with you. No more searching in the junk drawers or out in the garage. Just grab the kit to fix the "owies" around your house.

# HVAC Reminders for the Forgetful

It's hard to keep track of the furnace maintenance schedule. To make it easier, stick a small white magnetic board to your furnace duct. Write down the furnace filter size, the brand, the date you last changed the filter, and the date your furnace was last cleaned and checked. When it's time to put in a new filter or have the furnace cleaned, erase the old date and write down the new one.

# Shop Vacuum Drain Cleaner

Some drain clogs are just stubborn—drain cleaner is useless and a snake might scratch the tub. Here's a perfect solution: Stick the hose of a wet/dry shop vacuum down the drain, and the clog will be history in no time. If the hose fits loosely in the drain, you can seal around it with a rag.

# DON'T JUST STAND THERE– SHUT IT OFF!

An overflowing toilet can wreck the floor as well as the ceiling below, so don't let it happen! Next time you see the water in a stopped-up toilet preparing to breach the rim, calmly reach behind the toilet and shut off the valve that feeds the tank. The water will stop instantly, and you'll prevent a toxic waste cleanup project.

## FISH FOR LEAVES IN YOUR POND

If you have trees growing over your pond, falling leaves and seed pods will make a mess of your crystal-clear water. Just use a fish landing net to catch the debris (and leave your koi where they are!). The water will drain right through the loosely woven netting, and the leaves will be ready to dump.

# Keep Pond Pumps from Clogging

Filters on small outdoor pond pumps can clog quickly with leaves and debris from nearby plants. You can keep your pump flowing freely for longer just by enclosing it in a simple filter made from fiberglass screen mesh. Wrap the pump loosely with a square of mesh, then close the top with a zip tie or piece of wire. When you notice the water flow weakening, just rinse the gunk off the screen.

# Clog Stopper for Snow Blowers

Wet, heavy snow can build up in your snow blower chute, causing it to clog. To stop that from happening, try applying Rain-X glass cleaner to the inside of the chute. Works like a charm!

## NO-MESS OIL CHANGES

When you're draining the oil from a lawn mower, it's hard to direct the flow where you want it. Just fold a piece of cardboard for an easy, no-mess trough.

# EASY-SQUEEZE OIL

Pouring oil into a car, lawn mower or motorcycle can get messy. Here's a simple and tidy way to get the job done without using a funnel. Just reuse a pull-up stopper from a plastic water bottle. These come in a variety of sizes, so it's easy to find one that fits any oil container.

## Blow Out Your Hoses

If you don't drain all the water from your garden hoses before winter, ice can form and expand inside, causing hoses to rupture. To prevent this disaster, take a short length of old garden hose and attach a male air hose fitting. Now connect the fitting to your air compressor and quickly blow all the water out of your hoses. Make sure the other end of your garden hose is outside so you don't get water all over your garage floor.

# Snake Spouts

Your plumber's snake is a perfect tool for pulling clumps of wet leaves out of clogged downspouts.

## WHEELBARROW LEAF TRAPPER

Moving leaves in a wheelbarrow is no fun. A couple of good bounces and your leaves are all over the ground again. To combat this, take a 4-ft. piece of wire mesh fence and bend it around the top and sides of the wheelbarrow. Now you can load the wheelbarrow full of leaves and have them stay put as you wheel them to the compost pile.

## BIRDSEED CATCHER

To stop wasting birdseed and to keep it off the deck or out of the grass, screw a plastic plant saucer onto the bottom of your bird feeder. You'll catch most of the seeds that those slovenly, wasteful birds kick out. Those seeds can cause a real mess, especially when they start sprouting. And to avoid cooking up a dish of birdseed mush, cut a slit or two in the plastic for drainage.

## Tippy Baths Aren't for the Birds

To keep your birdbath level, install a level paver stone underneath it. Dig a hole about 2 in. deeper than the thickness of the paver and pack the loose soil to prevent settling. Spread and roughly level a 2-in. layer of sand in the hole. Set the paver on the sand and check it with a level. Lift one edge of the paver, and add or remove sand to level it.

## Ouchless Rose Deadheading

Deadheading roses can be a real pain if the thorns prick through your gloves. For ouch-free deadheading, use long-handled tongs to hold each rose head while you snip it off with your other hand. This process is also easier on your back and cuts the deadheading time in half.

## BACK-SAVING FERTILIZER FUNNEL

A large yard with a lot of shrubs means a lot of fertilizing and a lot of strain on your back to get the fertilizer near the root zones. To make this chore easier, duct-tape a funnel to a length of PVC pipe and then slit some holes in a plastic coffee container and clamp it to the pipe. Now just fill the container with fertilizer and move the pipe from shrub to shrub. The fertilizer will go right where you need it and you won't have to fight your way to the bases of dense shrubs—or spend the night lying on a heating pad.

# HIDE CONCRETE REPAIRS

Caulk repairs in concrete stand out like neon lights. However, if you sprinkle ordinary play sand on the wet caulk, the patch will blend in much better. Sprinkle the sand immediately after caulking, before it skins over, and then brush off the excess once the caulk dries.

## Roof Gripper

An old foam cushion from a sofa or chair not only saves your knees but also grips asphalt shingles to keep you from sliding down a steep pitch. It won't prevent falls, though, so it's not a substitute for safety equipment like a harness and roof jacks.

## Soft Sapling Protection

When you plant a new tree, wrap the trunk with a piece of foam pipe insulation before you attach the support wire. The foam is already split, so it's easy to wrap around the trunk. Then twist the wire around the foam and around the stake. This way, the wire won't cut into the sapling's fragile bark.

# NO-SWEAT FENCE POST PULLING

To remove a stubborn 4x4 fence post, fasten a 2x4 vertically to the post with five or six screws. Set a car jack on a board or block underneath the 2x4, and jack the post right out of the hole.

# TRASH BAG HOOP

Putting stuff in a trash bag can be very tough when the wind keeps blowing the bag closed. To hold the bag open, try using a 14-in. wooden embroidery hoop. It's just the right size for a 13-gallon kitchen trash bag. You can find an embroidery hoop at a hobby and craft store for about $5.

# Seal Outdoor Furniture Feet

Wooden outdoor furniture rots from the ground up, and the parts that touch the ground are usually end grain, which makes matters even worse. End grain readily wicks moisture. Moisture always wins in the end, but you can extend the life of your outdoor furniture by coating the feet with two-part epoxy. Be sure the feet you're coating are dry before applying the epoxy, and allow it to fully cure according to the instructions on the package. Then put your furniture back into use outside.

## Protect Saw Blades

For a quick way to protect the carbide teeth of your saw blade, cut a length of split wire loom to length and wrap it around your blade.

## SOLO DRYWALL HANGING

Make hanging drywall by yourself easier by creating a simple bracket with a couple of 16d nails between 1 and 2 ft. from each end of the sheet. Sink the nails into the studs 48-1/2 in. down from the ceiling and about 1 in. deep. Hoist the sheet and rest the bottom edge on the nails. Push the sheet up against the ceiling with one hand, and tack it into place with the other using a few prestarted drywall nails.

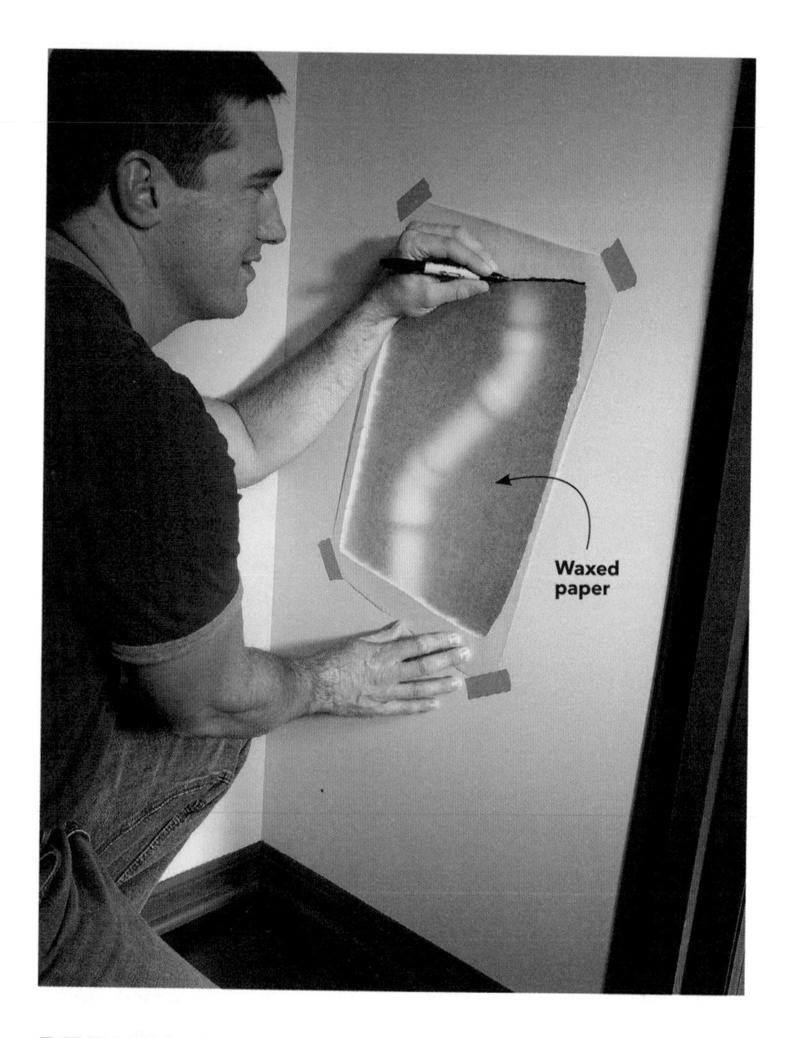


## PERFECT WALL PATCH EVERY TIME

When you have to patch a hole in a wall, instead of squaring it up or struggling to get exact measurements, just trace the hole on waxed paper to use as a guide. Tape waxed paper over the hole and run a permanent marker around the edges of the hole. Cut the waxed paper, tape it to the new drywall and cut the shape out of the drywall.

## Diverter Lube

Over time, hard water can leave deposits in the moving parts of your plumbing. If your tub spout diverter clogs, use WD-40. Curve the spray nozzle up the spout to the diverter valve. A couple of sprays will get things loosened and working again.

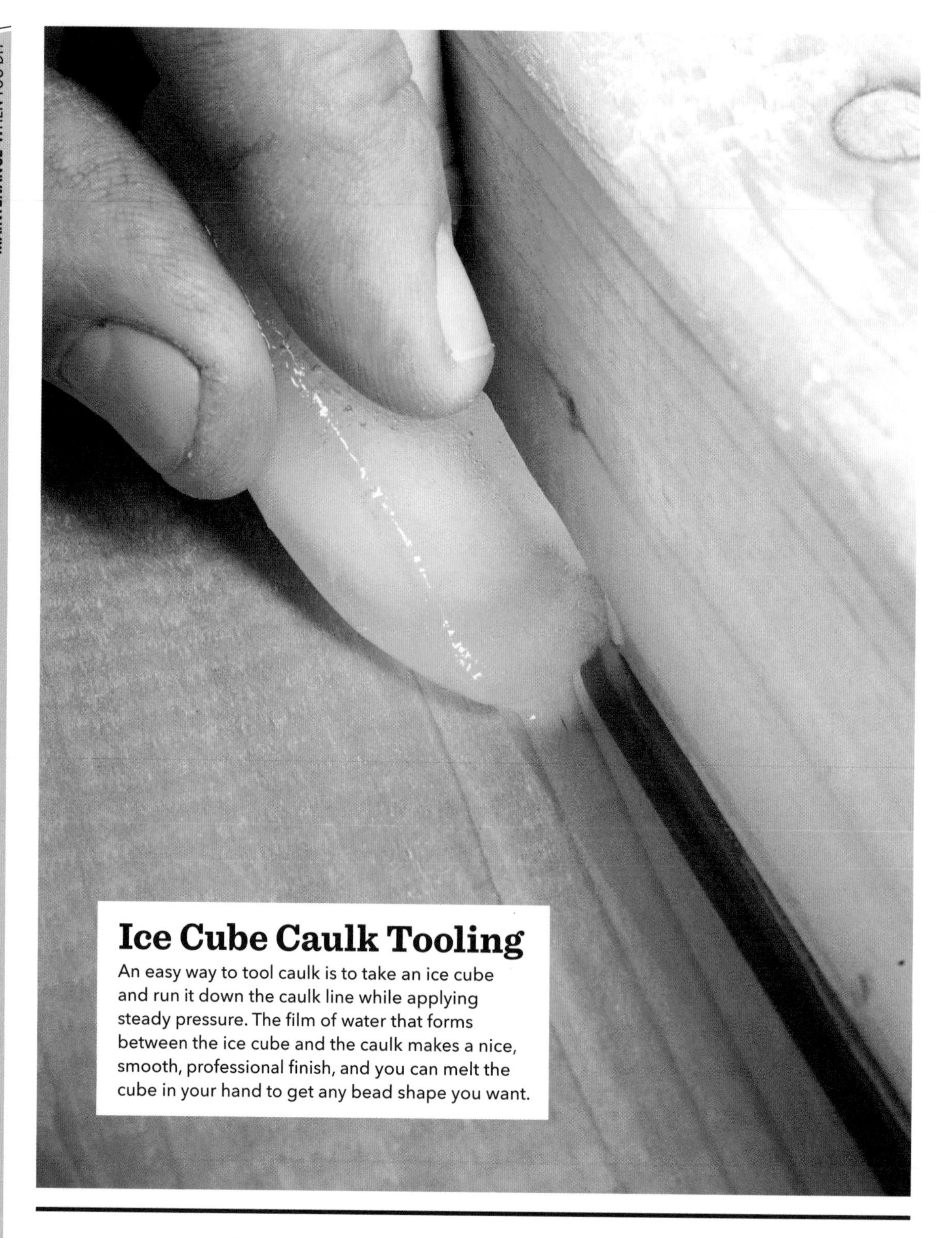

## Ice Cube Caulk Tooling

An easy way to tool caulk is to take an ice cube and run it down the caulk line while applying steady pressure. The film of water that forms between the ice cube and the caulk makes a nice, smooth, professional finish, and you can melt the cube in your hand to get any bead shape you want.

# EASY DRYWALL PATCHES FOR BIG HOLES

Doorknob-sized holes in drywall can take a lot of time to patch. Here's a way to make the repair quicker and easier. Make sure to remove any loose paper or drywall chunks around the hole before you patch it.

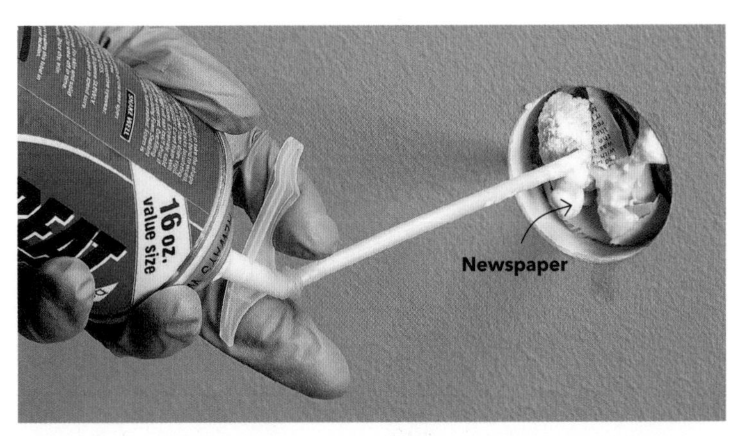


**1** Stuff newspaper loosely into the hole, and spray expanding insulating foam into the hole to give the patch more stability.

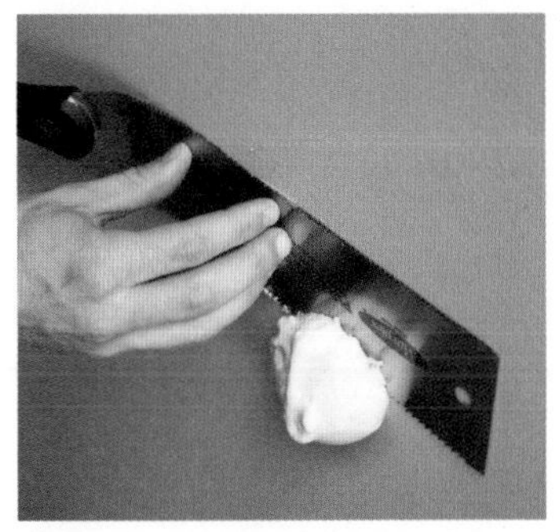

**2** After the foam dries, use a pull saw to cut it off. Then sand it flush with the wall.

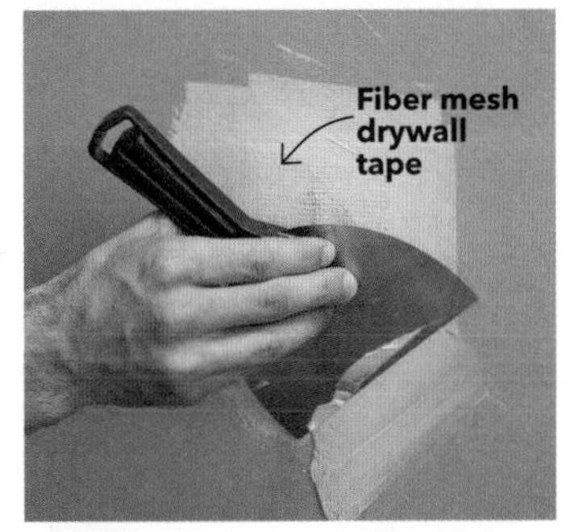


**3** Apply fiber mesh drywall tape that is cut slightly larger than the hole, and use joint compound for patching.

# FILL HOLES WITH DRYWALL ANCHORS

If you have holes in your wall from large nails or old anchors, make fillings go faster by screwing in drywall anchors first. Sink the heads just below the surface of the drywall—locking the anchors tightly into the wall—then fill them with surfacing compound. Sand the surface flat after it dries. If the holes already have screw-in anchors, leave them in place and just sink the heads a bit more.

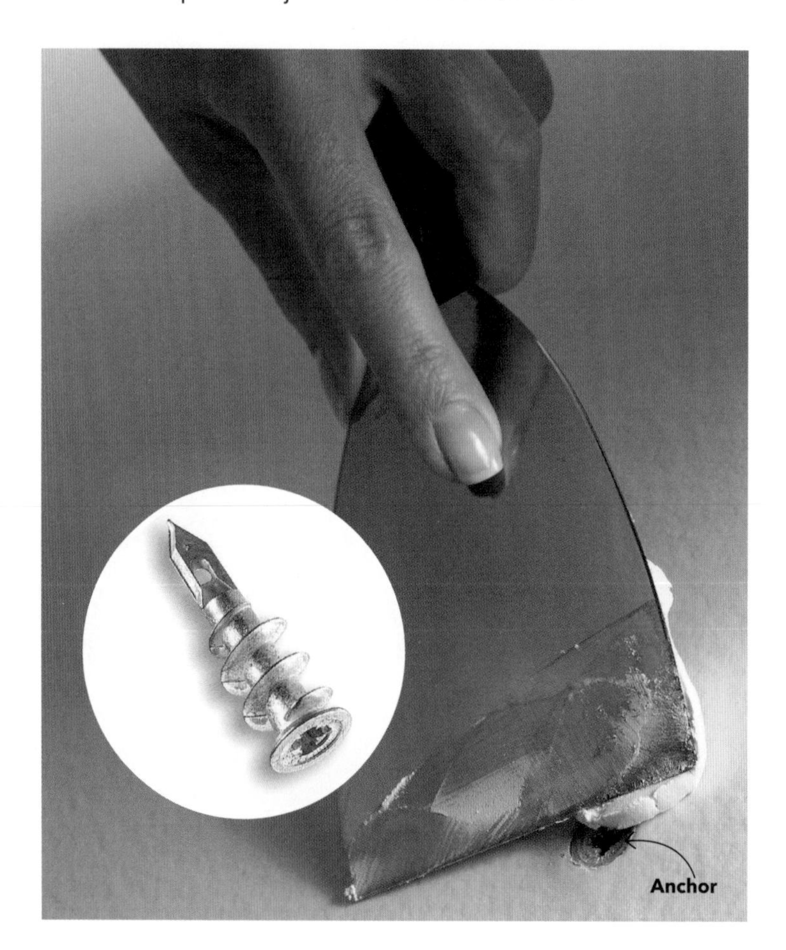

## Stop Lumber from Warping

If you store lumber in a pile, it's bound to twist and bow. That's one reason lumber loads are stored with steel banding. Use this same idea to stack your lumber. Wrap the ends with rope and use a narrow board to twist it tight, like a tourniquet. Screw down the narrow board to the top board on the pile until you're ready to work on your project.

# Finish Six Sides of a Door at Once

Staining or sealing a door takes a while if you set it on sawhorses to do one side and then let it dry before flipping it over to do the other. Cut the drying time in half by hanging two chains from the open joists in your garage and putting an S-hook on each of the ends. Hang the door by sliding the hooks through the door's hinge leaves or barrels. Now you can stain the entire door at one time.

## MARK STRAIGHT LINES ON ROUND PIPES

It's not easy to cut a straight line all the way around a pipe with a tin snips or a hacksaw. You can make the job a lot easier by marking a perfect cutting line with a square piece of cardboard or stiff paper. Just align the edges of the cardboard, pull it tight around the pipe and mark the edge all the way around. As long as you follow the line, your cut will be perfectly straight.

# POINTING BRICK

## Restore crumbling mortar joints with a chisel, a grinder and a lot of patience

**BRICK IS ONE OF THE MOST** prized exteriors for homes because it's attractive and quite easy to maintain. Yet, over the years seasonal expansion and contraction, water and ice all attack the solid mass of a brick wall at its most elastic (and weakest) point: the mortar joints.

Mortar joints deteriorate wherever water can soak them—under windows and walls, around chimneys, behind downspouts, at ground level and at any exposed wall top.

Repairing eroding and cracked mortar joints is called pointing, repointing or tuck-pointing. We'll show you the proper tools and techniques to repair and restore cracked, worn-away mortar joints to make them solid, durable and good looking. To keep them that way for the long run, you will have to stop water from getting into your bricks and into your foundation.

### IS THIS A JOB FOR YOU?

Repointing brick is slow, painstaking work that requires few special skills but an abundance of of patience. Using the steps we show in **Photos 1- 8**, you can expect to repoint about 20 sq. ft. of brickwork a day. However, if you rush and do careless work on a highly visible area, the results are sure to stick out like graffiti. Brick is durable; bad results will bother you for a long time! If you don't have pointing experience, you should consider hiring a pro for:

- Larger-scale pointing jobs, such as a whole wall that needs repair
- Chimney and wall repair requiring setting up and moving scaffolding
- Areas with a lot of loose or missing brick requiring rebuilding walls or corners
- Color-matching new mortar to existing mortar in highly visible areas

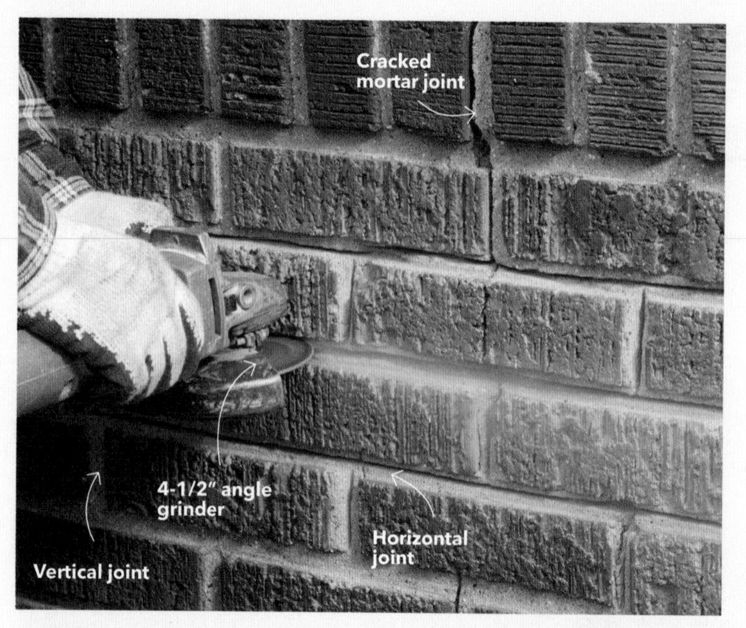


**1** Cut grooves 3/4 to 1 in. deep in cracked or deteriorating mortar using a 4-1/2 in. angle grinder fitted with a diamond blade. Push the blade into the joint until the grinder head contacts the brick, and make a single pass along the center of the joints.

**2** Position a flat utility chisel at the edge of the brick, and drive chisel toward the relief cut to fracture and remove the mortar.

## TOOLS AND MATERIALS

All materials necessary for this project should be easy to find. Home centers and well-stocked hardware stores carry tools and materials needed for pointing brick. Anything they don't have can be bought from retailers that sell to contractors.

Cleaning out old mortar joints requires basic tools you likely already have in your workshop: a hammer, a flat utility chisel **(Photo 2)**, a pair of good safety glasses, a dust mask and a whisk broom. Filling the cleaned-out joints requires masonry tools: a brick trowel **(Photo 5)**, a 3/8-in. pointing trowel **(Photo 5)**, a special tool for contouring the joints **(Photo 7)** and a pair of waterproof gloves.

If you do tackle larger jobs or encounter hard mortar that can't be easily chiseled out, we recommend that you rent or buy an angle grinder fitted with a diamond blade **(Photo 1)**. Select a grinder with a 4-1/2-in. blade diameter; larger grinders are harder to control and cut the mortar too deep.

## BREAK OUT THE OLD MORTAR

Break out the old mortar using a hammer and cold chisel or a flat utility chisel that's narrow enough to fit into the joints **(Photo 2)**. Wear safety glasses and a dust mask and remove 3/4 to 1 in. of the old mortar (more if needed) until you end up with a solid base for bonding the new mortar.

If the mortar is so soft that the bricks are loosening up, you'll have to remove and properly reset them. If the cracked mortar is harder, make a relief cut down

**3** Clean out all the loose dust from the brick cavity using a whisk broom or compressed air. Moisten the cleaned cavity with a garden hose.

**4** Dump mortar mix into a cement boat and gradually add the specified amount of water while mixing with a brick trowel. Allow the mortar to rest for 10 minutes, then remix it before using. The mix is ready when it sticks to an overturned trowel.

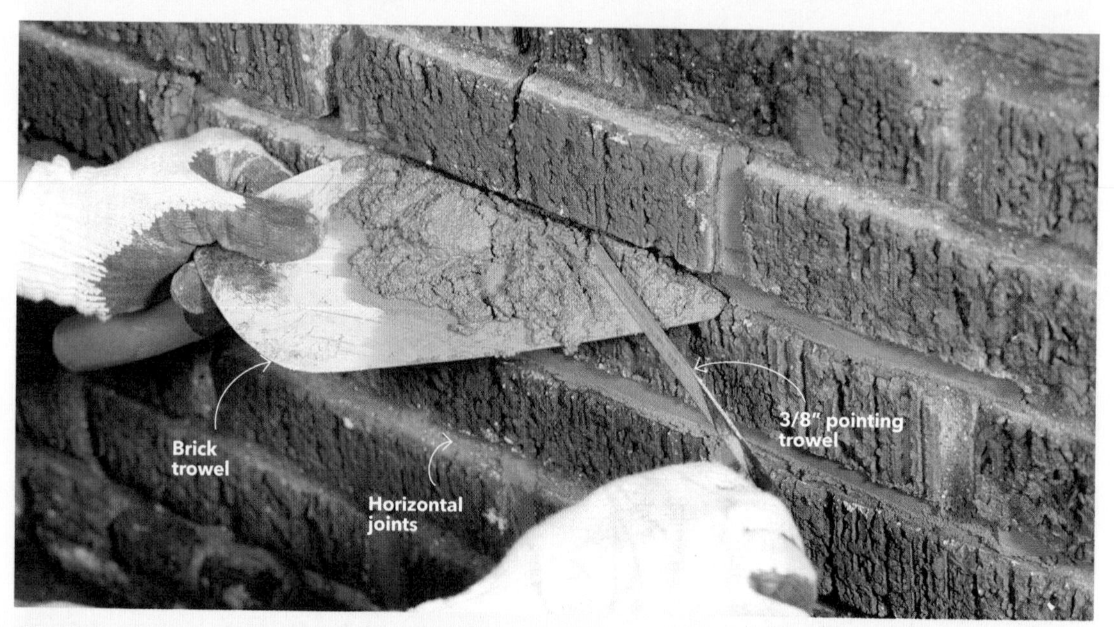


**5** Load mortar onto an overturned brick trowel, hold the trowel under the horizontal joint–tight to the brick–and sweep 1/4-in. slivers of mortar into the cavity using a 3/8-in.-wide pointing trowel. Fill the horizontal joints first. Avoid getting mortar on the brick face.

the center of the mortar joint using the pointed edge of the chisel and then gently chip out the mortar that contacts the brick. If the removal work is going really slowly, use an angle grinder to make the relief cuts **(Photos 1 and 2)**. Exercise care here; the grinder can easily nick and chip the bricks, so don't use it to clean out the mortar contacting the brick. To avoid nicking the bricks, cut the vertical joints before cutting the horizontal joints.

Once the old mortar has been removed, dust the joints **(Photo 3)**. Prepare joints to receive new mortar by misting them lightly with a garden hose sprayer.

### MIX THE MORTAR JUST RIGHT

Using only the amount of water specified by the manufacturer, mix the mortar until it's the consistency of peanut butter and sticky enough to cling to an overturned trowel **(Photo 4)**. It should be stiff but not crumbly.

Allow the mortar to "rest" for 10 minutes as it absorbs the water, then remix it using your brick trowel. Don't try to revive mortar that's drying out by adding more water to it. Mix a fresh batch instead.

### FILLING THE MORTAR JOINTS

Follow the pointing techniques shown in **Photos 5 and 6** and these additional tips:

- Pack mortar tightly with no voids for the strongest joints.
- Fill deeper joints (greater than 3/4 in.) in two stages. Allow the first layer to partially harden (until a thumbprint barely leaves an indentation) before adding the second layer.

**6** **Load smaller amounts of mortar onto the back of the brick trowel, hold the trowel tip along the vertical joints and above the horizontal joints–tight to the brick–then sweep and pack the mortar into the cavity using the pointing trowel.**

- In hot weather, work in shaded areas first (if possible) so the mortar doesn't dry too fast. Mix smaller batches of mortar.
- Don't work in temperatures below 40 degrees F.
- Match new joints with the old.
- Buy the mortar finishing tool you need to match the contour and depth of your existing mortar joints **(Figure A)**.
- We recommend that you repoint brick sills **(Photo 1)** and other horizontal brick surfaces (ledges, wall tops, etc.) with flush joints **(Figure A)** to promote drainage–regardless of the type of mortar joint in your vertical walls.
- Allow the mortar to cure to "thumbprint" hardness before you finish the joint. Shape the vertical joints before working the long horizontal joints.
- Use a soft-bristle brush as shown in **Photo 8** to remove mortar chunks on the brick face before they harden. The brush keeps the mortar from smearing. If you do smear mortar onto the brick, you'll have to go back later and use a chemical cleaner.
- Prevent water from entering and damaging the brickwork by applying color-matched polyurethane caulk where stucco, wood and other materials meet brick.

**7** **Drive a 6d box nail into a short 1x2 board so that it matches the depth of the existing joints. To "rake" the joints, hold the board perpendicular to the bricks and move it back and forth, first along the vertical joints and then the horizontal joints. Other joint profiles require other shaping tools.**

**8** **Sweep the loose mortar from the finished joints and brick faces using a soft-bristle brush. To help the new mortar harden, mist it twice a day for two days using a hand pump sprayer or a light mist from a garden hose.**

**FIGURE A**
**COMMON MORTAR JOINT PROFILES**

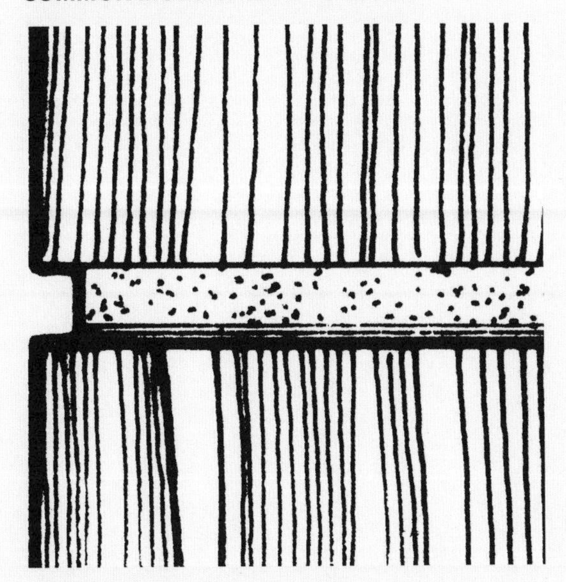

**RAKED JOINT**
Formed by removing mortar to 1/4 in. deep with a raking block **(Photo 7)**.

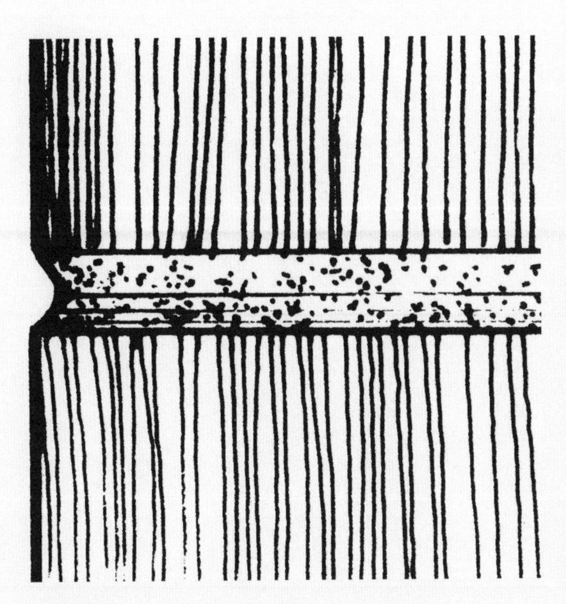

**V-JOINT**
Formed by a brick jointer, it has a concave V look.

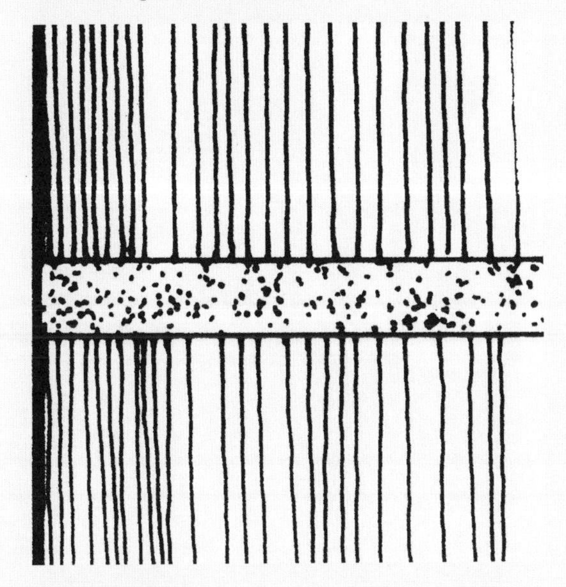

**FLUSH JOINT**
Formed by cutting off the mortar with the edge of a brick trowel.

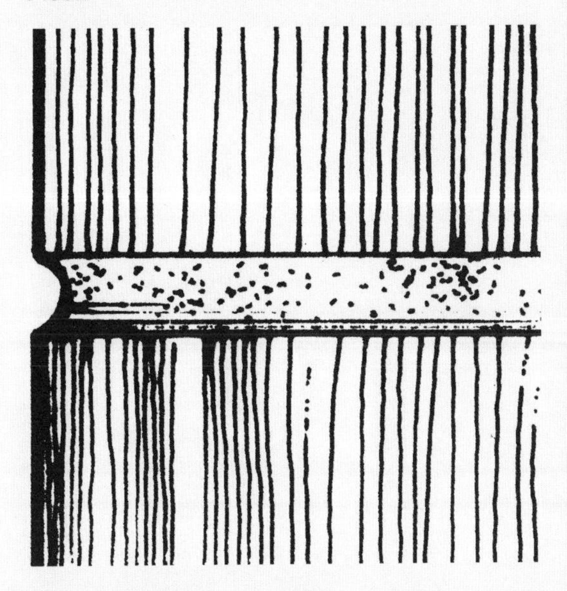

**CONCAVE JOINT**
Formed by the curved end of a brick jointer.

CHAPTER 4

# TOOLS & TECHNIQUES

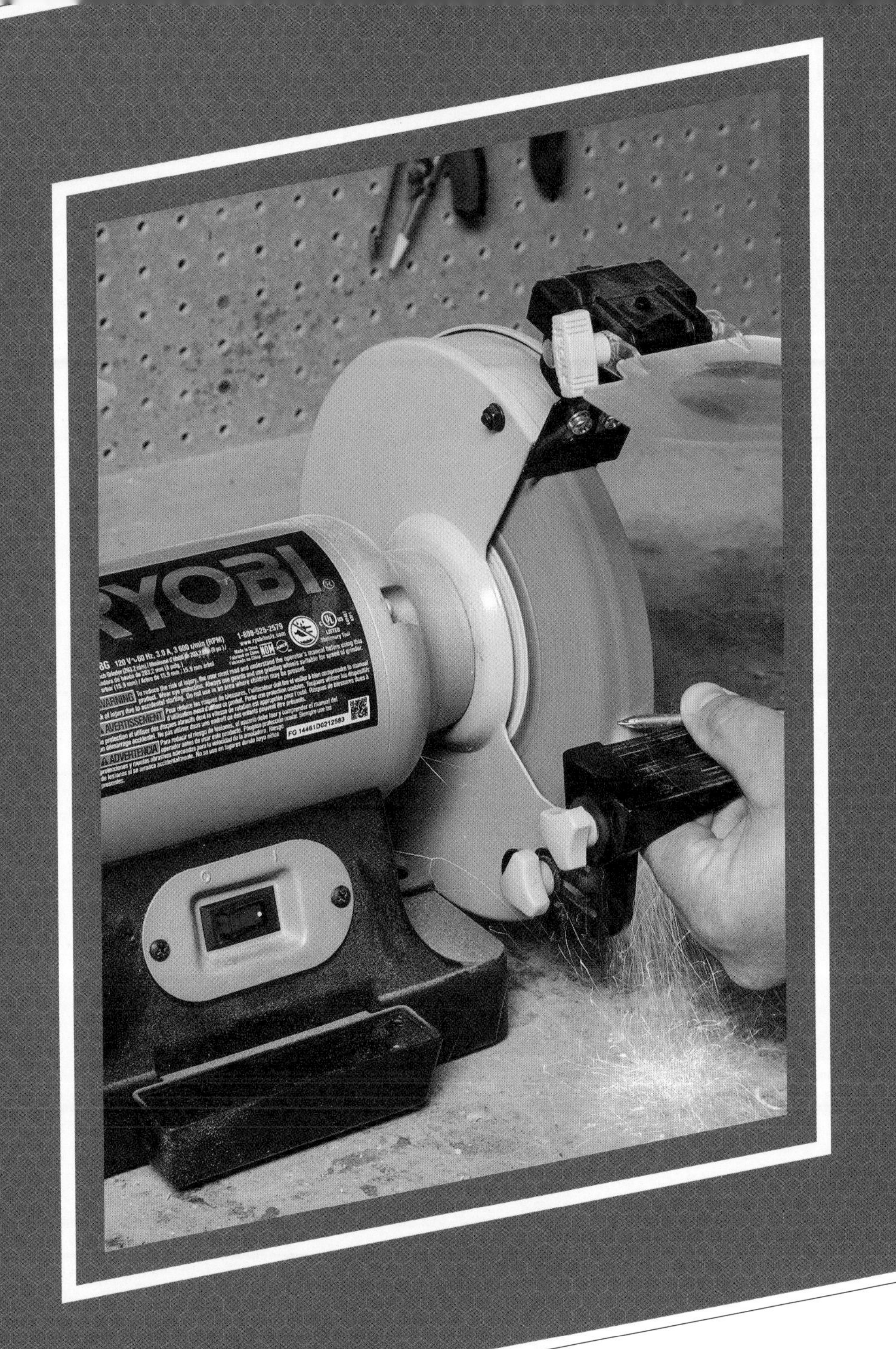
RYOBI
WARNING
AVERTISSEMENT
ADVERTENCIA

## TAKE YOUR GLUE FOR A SPIN

If you don't like waiting for wood glue to come out after you squeeze the bottle, put the cap on and swing it around a couple of times. Centrifugal force will concentrate the glue at the top of the bottle, making it come out of the nozzle faster.

## Installing Flooring in Tight Spots

When installing wood flooring in the cramped corners of a closet, it can be tough to hold the last edge and corner pieces to glue them in. For a solution to the problem, use duct tape to make "handles" for the planks, to pull the pieces together. Then stick the tape onto the adjoining plank to act as a clamp while the glue dries.

## Clever Lug Wrench Twofer

Changing a flat tire isn't fun, and spending any extra time on the side of the road increases the safety hazard. Make this task a little bit easier with these two tips: Mark the correct socket for your vehicle with electrical tape. If you use the same wrench for different vehicles (or your boat), color-code the appropriate sockets. The second tip is to cover the unused socket arms with foam pipe insulation. This will make the whole ordeal easier on your hands.

# Lawn Chemical Overspray Prevention

To protect your shrubs and flowers when using a weed killer such as Roundup, use this nifty technique. Take the sprayer head off your spray wand, tape a funnel to the wand and then replace the sprayer head. The funnel directs the weed killer where you want it and protects everything else from overspray.

## NUTTY STAIN MIXER

Pigment in stain settles to the bottom of the can and forms a hard sludge that requires a lot of stirring before it dissolves. For faster mixing, just drop in two or three nuts, press the cover back on and shake—but don't use this trick with polyurethane or varnish, since it creates air bubbles.

## PULL-TAB PICTURE FRAME HOOK

If you're hanging pictures and run out of those sawtooth hangers, just grab the nearest pop can. Bend the pull tab back and forth until it breaks off, then screw it to your picture frame. Bend the free end out slightly and hang the picture.

# Spring-Loaded Pliers

If you can't manipulate your pliers with one hand in tight quarters, here's what to do: Press the ends of a short length of vinyl tubing over the handles to hold them open. Squeeze to close. PS: Take your pliers to the hardware store or home center to get tubing that's a perfect fit.

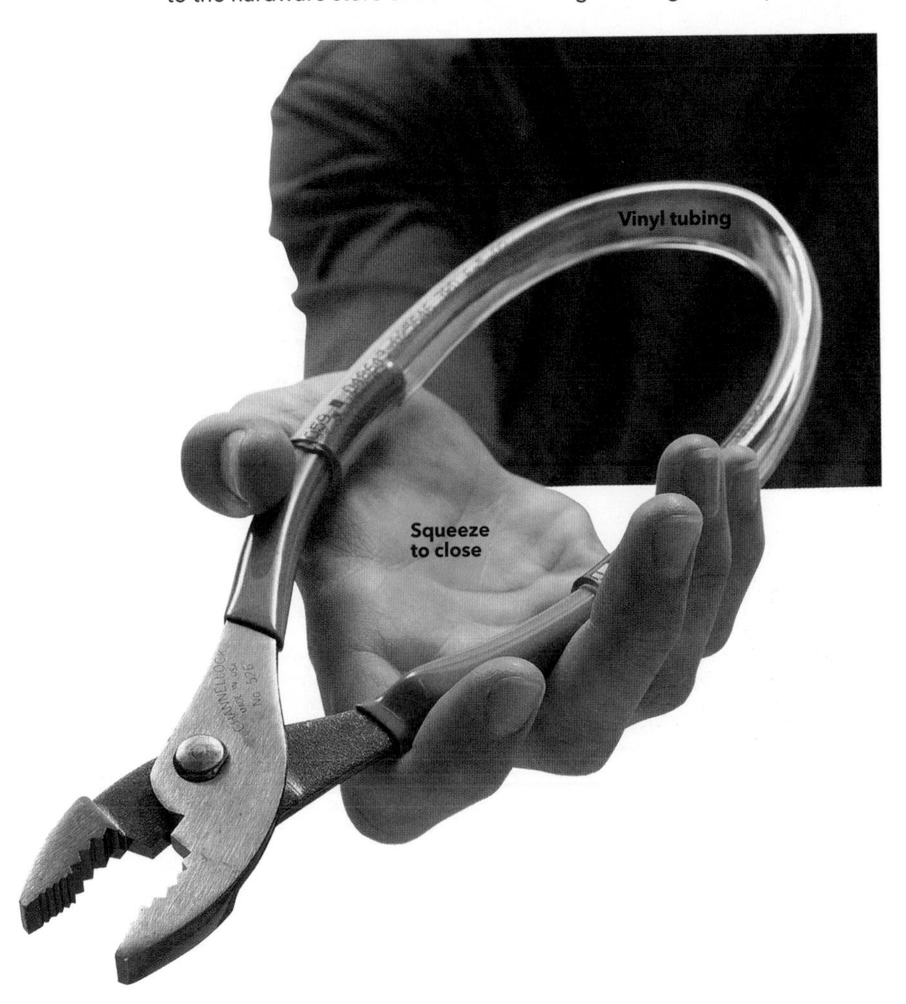

# Easy Nailing in Awkward Spots

Nailing small fasteners in hard-to-reach spots can be really frustrating, especially for people with large hands. For a simple solution, poke a fastener through a foam brush. You can hold the brush handle while you hammer the nail home, then just pull the foam end free through the nail head. Easy, cheap and effective!

# NO-FADE CHALK LINES

Always start a tile-laying job by snapping a series of layout chalk lines on the area to be covered, then spray the lines with a clear coat of polyurethane. That way you can walk on the lines or sweep over them and they won't fade or disappear.

## STAY-PUT DOWNSPOUT EXTENSIONS

Before mowing the lawn, it's a good idea to fold up downspouts so you can mow those areas efficiently. Sometimes that creates an issue because a good breeze can blow them back down. Here's a simple solution: Put a small square of hook-and-loop tape where each extension and vertical section meet. Now when you flip an extension up, it'll stay up.

# Smoother Varnishing

Here's a neat tip you can use to get a super smooth finish when building or refinishing furniture. Open the can of varnish and put it in a few inches of warm water. Let it sit for about 10 minutes, giving it a stir every few minutes. Stir it again right before you apply it. It will flow more easily, penetrate more thoroughly and set up better. This also works for tung and other penetrating oils.

# Picture-Hanging Perfection

When you're hanging a group of pictures, it can be hard to visualize exactly where everything should go. Try this next time: Lay the pictures out on the floor. Get them arranged just how you like them. Then flip them over and make a little diagram of your grouping. Measure the distance of each picture's hanger from the adjacent walls, and jot it down on your diagram. Transfer those hanger locations to the wall and you'll have a perfect grouping every time.

## DRYWALL KNIFE PROTECTOR

This nifty solution keeps the fine edges of your drywall knives from getting dinged. Buy 3/8-in. clear tubing at the hardware store and cut lengths to fit the blades. Then take a sharp utility knife, slit the tubing lengthwise and slip the tubing over each blade. The tubing is somewhat clingy, so it stays put even in a toolbox tote.

## NUT + NUT = BOLT HEAD

Hanger bolts are tricky to install. One end is threaded for wood, the other end has machine threads and there's no head. To make it easier, thread two nuts on the machine-thread end and tighten them against each other. This allows you to use a wrench for installation.

## Easy Concrete Mixing

Skip the concrete mixer rental. Instead, use two people, a 6 x 6-ft. heavy-duty tarp with rope handles at each corner, and a water bucket. Pour a bag of concrete mix in the center of the tarp, make a crater in the center and add the recommended amount of water. Each person grabs two tarp corners as if going to fold the tarp. Lift one corner at a time going in one direction, as if doing "the wave," and continue for a minute or two until the bag is mixed. Pour the concrete from the tarp into the form and start a new bag.

## Itch Remover

A sticky lint roller pulls those nasty insulation fibers off your skin and clothes—and reduces itching later.

## SEED ID

When you sow new seeds in the spring, it is hard to remember exactly where they were planted before they sprout. That's a big problem when putting in other seeds and plants, and even for watering, especially if you plant in curved rows. To make rows easy to find, sprinkle a little play sand over the seeds as you plant them. The seeds will sprout right through the sand, you'll know where to water and the sand will help keep the weeds down while providing good drainage.

## GROCERY BAG SHOE COVERS

When you're working outside, it never fails that you need to go into the house for something you forgot. If you don't feel like taking off your shoes, keep a stash of plastic grocery bags in the mudroom. Just step into the bags to cover your dirty shoes, and tie the handle loops around your ankles. Now you can go into the house without leaving a trace.

## UMBRELLA STAND/PLANTER

Many umbrella stands are designed for use under patio tables, which can make finding a stand-alone one tricky—but, thanks to this tip, not impossible. Purchase a large resin flowerpot and fill it about a third full with concrete. While the concrete is wet, insert a short length of PVC pipe just slightly larger in diameter than the umbrella pole (be sure to cover the bottom of the pipe with duct tape so the pipe won't fill with concrete). Then drill a few drainage holes above the concrete, fill the pot with potting soil and plant some shade-loving plants. Now you have a windproof umbrella stand and a beautiful pot of flowers in one!

# Long-Handled Shears

To cut tree branches that are just out of reach, extend the range of your lopping shears and gain leverage with this easy trick. Slip lengths of PVC pipe over the handles, tape the pipe in place and you'll have shears that reach out a few more feet for pruning.

# Mud Ladle

If you have the misfortune of experiencing a rainstorm soon after digging footing holes for a new shed, try this trick. To get rid of the water quickly so you can pour concrete, whip up a "mud ladle" out of a section of round ductwork, a piece of 3/4-in. plywood and a solid wood handle. Thanks to your new tool, you'll be able to scoop out all the irksome water in a few minutes.

## MEASURING STICK FOR FIREWOOD

For a tidy stack, you may prefer your firewood to be all the same length. The simplest measuring device is your chain saw's bar.

# STOP ROPES FROM UNRAVELING

Quickly and permanently repair fraying rope ends by covering them with the heat-shrink tubing used to seal splices in electrical wiring. Buy tubing with a slightly larger diameter than the rope, slip it over a freshly trimmed rope end and then heat it with a heat gun (or a hair dryer set on the highest temperature) until it shrinks tightly around the rope. You can find heat-shrink tubing in the electrical section of home centers and hardware stores or online.

## Planer Stand

It's not easy to plane long boards without an assistant, so mount your planer to a piece of plywood and bolt the plywood to a miter saw stand. The stand is equipped with adjustable supports that help you infeed and outfeed long boards when working alone.

# Mini Power Washer

A garden sprayer can be a mini power washer for cleaning windowsills and other hard-to-reach spots. Before you put water in the tank, be sure to rinse it repeatedly to flush out any chemical residue.

# GOT A LIGHT?

Many DIYers have a few small key chain flashlights just gathering dust in their shops—and these trinkets are perfect light sources for drilling in low-light areas. Blow the dust off those flashlights and glue a small magnet on each with epoxy. Attach the lights to all types of tools, including stationary ones like a drill press and a band saw, and you'll always have a light when you need it.

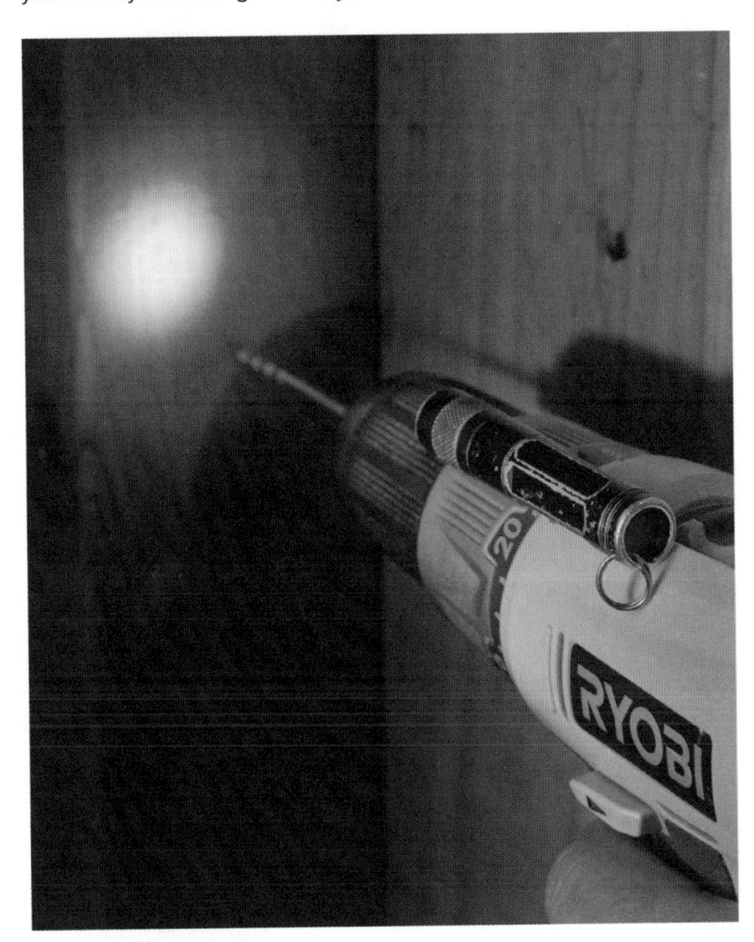

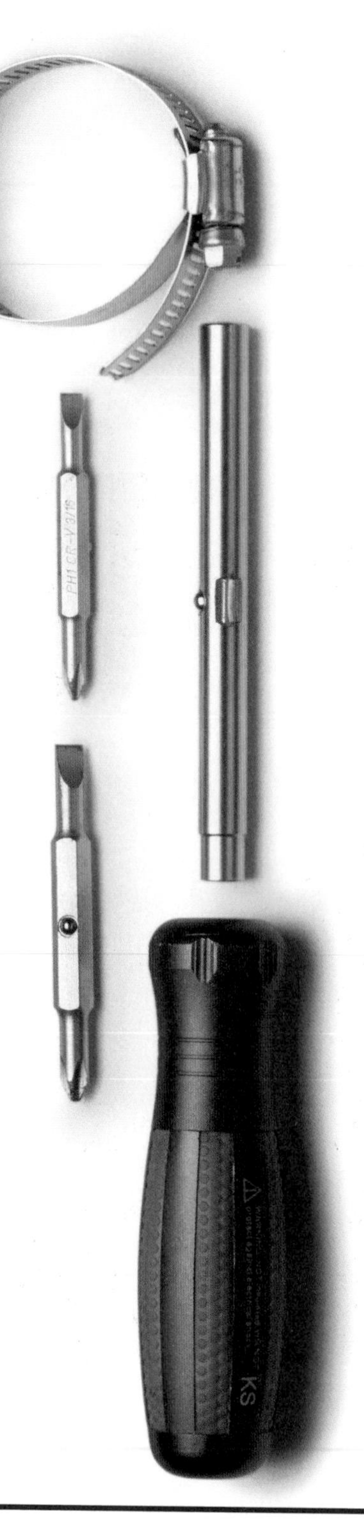


# BUILT-IN NUT DRIVERS

Useful combination screwdrivers with two Phillips head sizes and two slotted head drivers save you trips to the toolbox and back. When the drivers are pulled out, the two ends that hold the driver heads will also drive 1/4-in. and 5/16-in. bolt heads. These ends make perfect nut drivers for tightening and loosening hose clamps as well as appliance fasteners.

# Ironing Board Back-Saver

Working under the sink while on your back isn't exactly a pleasant experience, especially when the sharp cabinet edge cuts into your shoulder blades. Make it more comfortable by lying on an ironing board. Set one end of the board inside the cabinet and support the other end with a scrap piece of 2x4. It won't make the repair any easier, but it's definitely easier on your back!

## Tile Shower

Tile saws can kick out a lot of water every time you cut tile. To keep the front of your shirt dry, wear a trash bag as a vest. Cut three holes (for your head and arms) and slip it over your head. When done, dry it with a rag and store it with the tile saw.

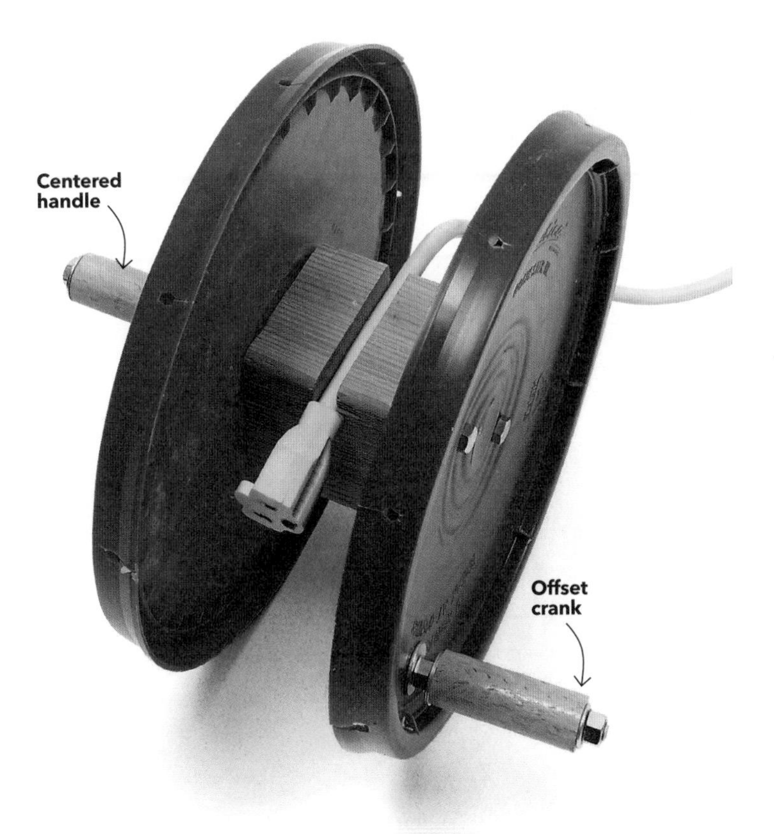


## BUCKET-LID CORD REEL

Make this handy cord reel using extra bucket lids from drywall mud pails or other 5-gallon buckets. Cut a 5-in. length of 4x4 and then cut a groove in the side just wide enough to fit your cord. Fasten the lids to the 4x4 with 1/4 x 2-in. lag screws. Make handles from an old 1-1/8-in.-diameter broom handle and drill a 1/2-in. hole through each handle center. Fasten the crank to the lid with bolts, nuts and washers, and apply Loctite sealant to the end nut. Fasten the handle to the 4x4 through the lid with a 6-1/2-in. lag screw. Then just insert your cord and reel it in.

## WRENCH CADDY

Organize the wrenches in your toolbox by stringing them onto a large, brightly colored carabiner. It will keep your wrenches together while also making them portable and easy to spot.

# Low-Cost, Lightweight 8-Ft. Level

A good 8-ft. level can be costly, but you can make a good substitute with just a steel stud and a 2- or 4-ft. level. Unlike wood, steel studs are always straight, and they weigh almost nothing. If your level is magnetic, you can stick it to the stud for vertical work.

# Comfortable Sawhorse Worktable

A higher worktable can be easier on your back than the standard height, and it's also pretty easy to make. First, measure how much higher than your sawhorses you want your work surface to be. Then cut notches in your four table legs at that height, and screw them to the sides of your sawhorses. Set a sheet of plywood on top, and you're all set.

# MAKE YOUR OWN AWL

To punch small holes in drywall for plastic screw anchors, use an awl. An awl pushes through easily, resulting in much less dust than drilling. Store-bought awls are usually too small for this task, so make your own by using a disc sander or bench grinder to grind a sharp tip onto the end of an old, worn-out screwdriver.

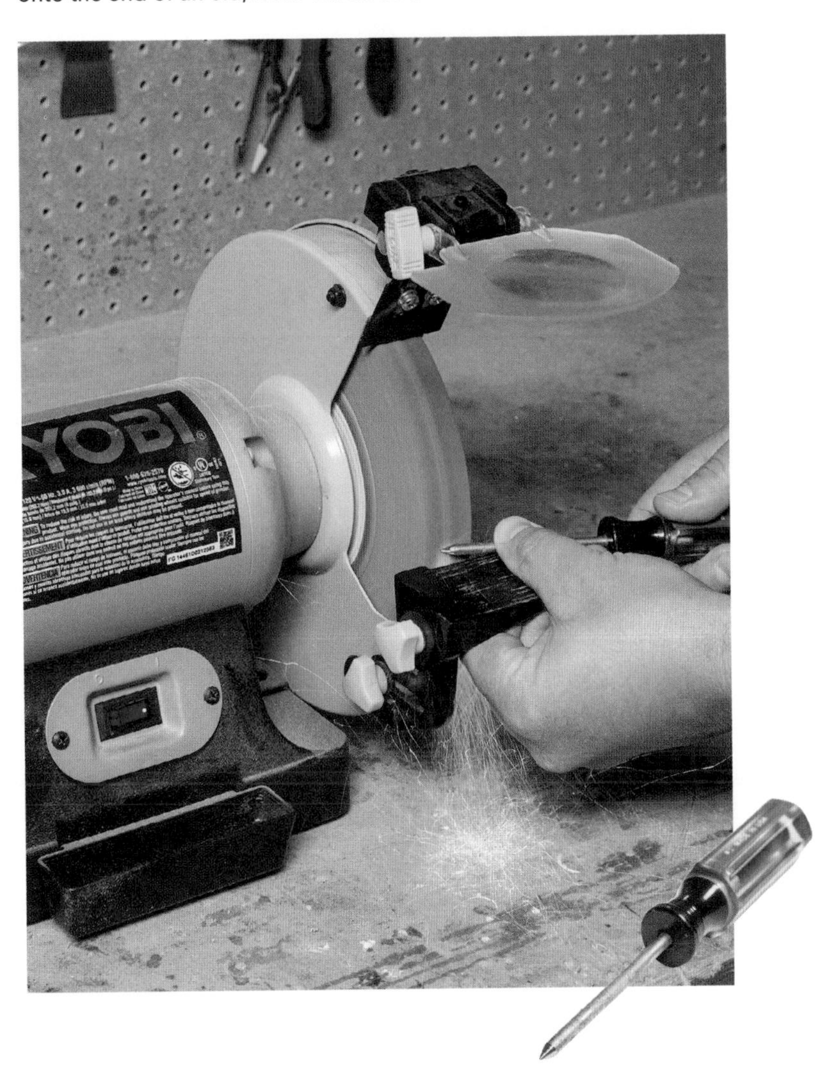

# HANDY DRY LUBRICANT

You can buy powdered graphite lubricant at a hardware store, but you already have it in a handy stick form in your pencil. Pencil "lead" is actually graphite and is less messy than powder.

## Spray Can Six-Pack

A cardboard six-pack corrals loose spray cans for a neater shop.

# Rolling Work Lamp

Get light wherever you need it by clipping your work light to your shop vacuum. A shop vacuum is the ideal height to shine light at the right angle, and since it's on wheels, you can pull it along to light even the darkest corners. Your temporary solution will become a permanent "fixture" on all your basement projects.

# MIXING BUCKET HOLDER

To hold a 5-gallon bucket for mixing a batch of mortar or drywall compound, create a "bucket vise" from a milk crate and wood. Screw the crate onto a piece of plywood. Secure the bucket in the crate by wedging in a scrap 2x4. With your feet firmly straddling the crate, you're ready for high-speed mixing!

# HANDY RAG CUTTER

You can recycle old T-shirts and towels to use as rags in your shop. To speed up the shirt-to-rag process, clamp a utility knife in your bench vise and make a cut to help tear the scraps. If you're careful, you can make the entire cut with the knife.

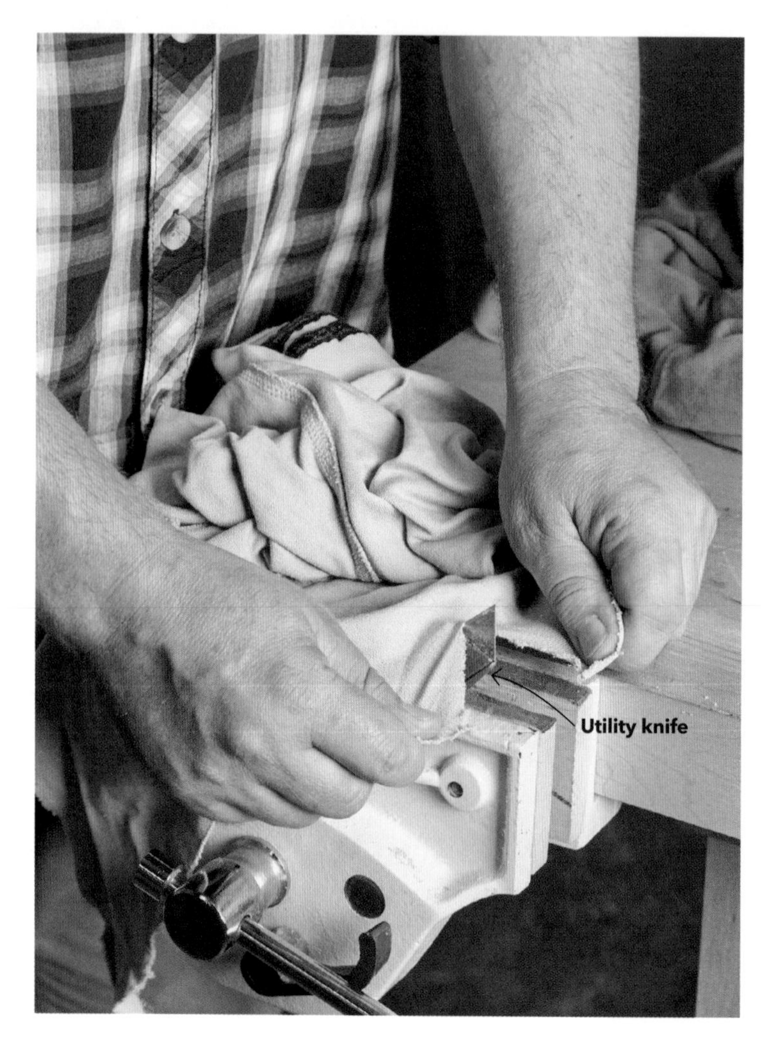

## Compressor Creeper

Air compressors are heavy and cumbersome to haul around a shop or garage, so put yours on wheels by placing it on a mechanic's creeper. It'll be a breeze to roll, rather than carry, your compressor wherever you need it.

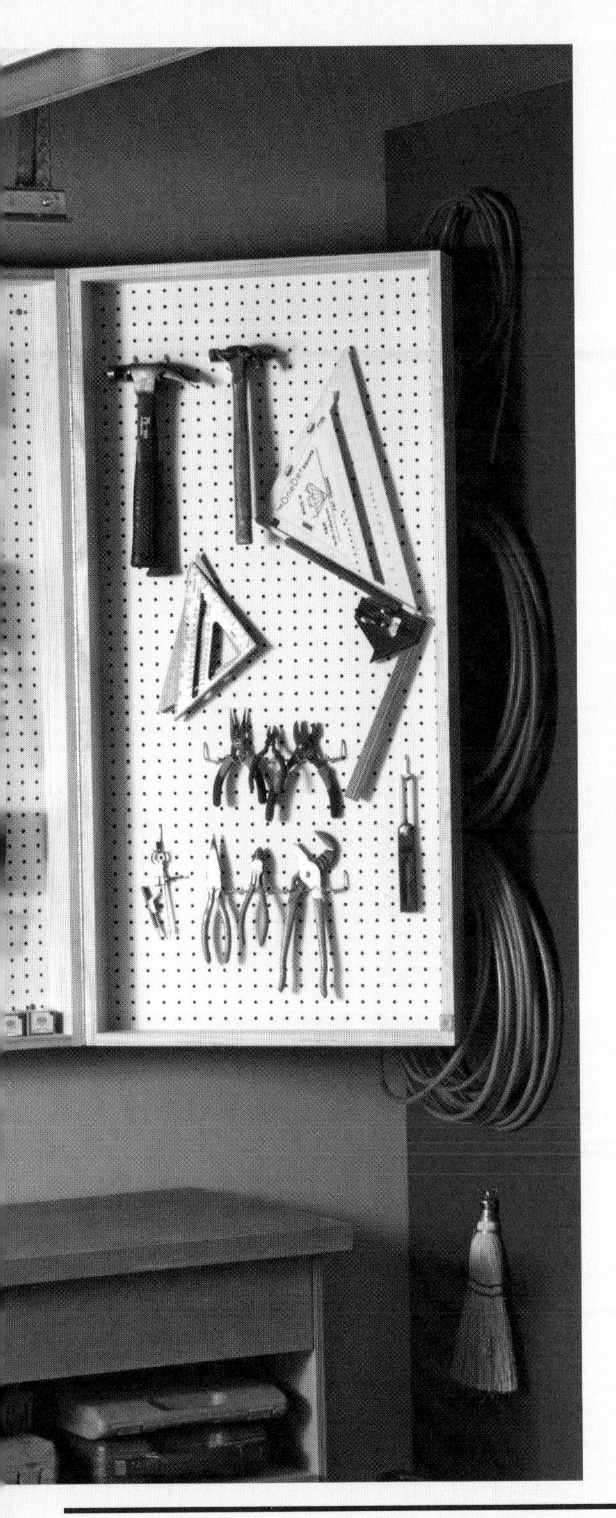

# COMPACT TOOL CABINET

## Build an easy-access pegboard storage unit

### BUILD THE BASE FRAME

Cut your 1x4 frame boards to size. We used a higher-grade pine. It was worth the extra cash to be able to work with straight, knot-free wood. Sand all the boards with 100-grit sandpaper before assembling the frames. We glued the joints and nailed them with 1-1/2-in. brads, just to hold them together. When the base was fully assembled, we came back and drove in two 2-in. trim-head screws. If you don't have a brad nailer, no problem; the screws are plenty strong on their own.

### ATTACH THE PEGBOARD TO THE BASE FRAME

We wanted solid material along all the edges, which meant we couldn't just measure 47-3/4 in. from the end of the sheet and assume the holes wouldn't be exposed. Not all sheets of pegboard are the same size, and sometimes the holes aren't perfectly centered on the sheet. We squared up the frame and held it in place with a couple of temporary cross braces and brads. We laid a half sheet of pegboard on top of the frame so all the rows of holes were inset at least 1/4 in. before fastening it down. Fasten the sheet with 1-in. brads every 8 in. or so **(Photo 1)**, and use glue on all unfinished sides of the pegboard.

Once the pegboard is secure, trim off the excess material with a router equipped with a flush-trim bit **(Photo 2)**. If you don't own a flush-trim bit, this is an excellent opportunity to spend $20 on a tool you'll definitely use again. Trimming down pegboard creates clouds of very fine dust, which seem to get into everything. We cut our first edge and then got smart and moved the whole operation outdoors.

**1 FASTEN PEGBOARD TO THE BASE FRAME.** **Attach temporary braces to hold the base frame perfectly square. Lay a 4 x 4-ft. sheet of pegboard over the frame. The oversized sheet lets you position the holes so they won't be along the outer edge of the cabinet. Note: If you don't have a router to trim off the excess pegboard (see Photo 2), position the pegboard, mark it with a pencil and cut it to size before nailing it in place.**

Don't even think about doing this without wearing a dust mask. If you don't have a router to trim off the excess, just mark the outline of the base frame onto the half sheet of pegboard and trim it with a saw.

## BUILD THE DOORS

Use the same process to build the door frames and install the door pegboard as you did for the base. Again, pay special attention to the spacing of the holes before you attach the pegboard and rout it flush. The only difference this time is that the first layer of pegboard should be facing down.

Once that layer of pegboard is in place, rip down 3/4-in. strips of wood to act as a spacer between the first and the second layers **(Photo 3)**. This will allow clearance for the peg hardware on both sides of the door. Align the spacers the same way you did with the frame, so the end grain cannot be seen from the sides. Tack them in place with 1-1/2-in. brads.

Tack on the outer layer of pegboard or dry-erase board (white/gloss hardboard panel) with 1-in. brads, and then drive in 2-in. trim-head screws about

**2 TRIM THE PEGBOARD FLUSH.** Install a flush-trim bit in your router and trim off the overhanging pegboard. Routing pegboard whips up a dust storm, so wear a mask.

**3 COMPLETE THE DOORS.** A 3/4-in. spacer between the two layers of pegboard creates space for the hooks.

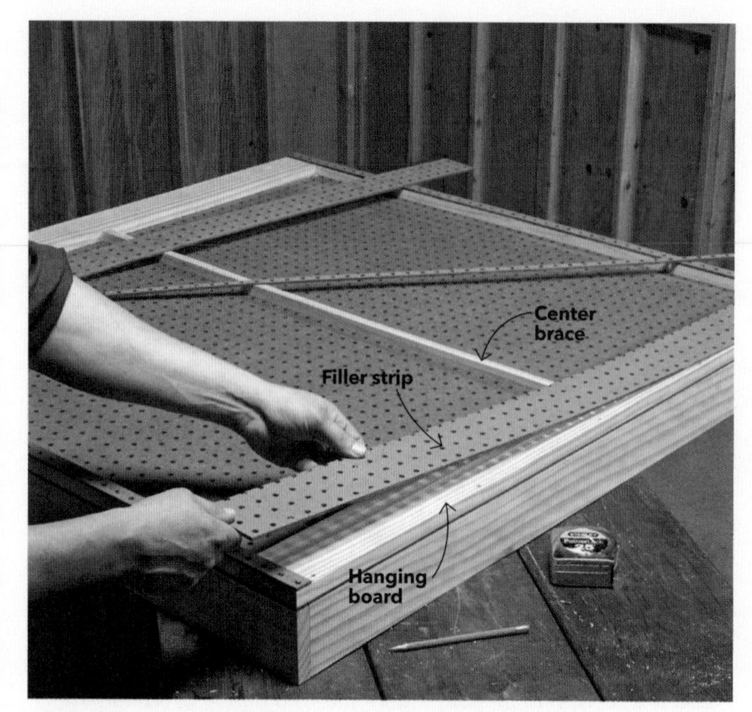


**4 ADD FILLER STRIPS.** Installing filler strips on the back of the base will allow the doors to open a little wider.

every 8 in. or so. Pegboard and other hardboard materials tend to pucker when you screw into them, so predrill the holes with a small countersink drill bit. Don't attach the screen mold on the outside of the doors until the doors are hung onto the base.

### FINISH THE BACK SIDE OF THE BASE

There needs to be space for the peg hardware on the back of the base, so install 3/4-in. strips of pine on the back two sides of the base. Fasten them with glue and 1-1/2-in. brads. Next, install a full pine 1x4 on the top and bottom of the back side of the base. These are the boards you will end up screwing through when you hang the cabinet on the wall. Glue and tack these boards into place, and then drive 2-in. trim-head screws through the boards into the base frame.

Use another 3/4-in. strip of pine to brace the center of the pegboard. Install this center brace between the holes. Secure it with glue and a few 1-in. brads from the front side of the base. This will prevent the 4 x 4-ft. sheet of pegboard from getting too floppy.

The doors will be thicker than the base once you add the screen molding. This means they'll make contact with the walls before they fully open. If you add filler strips of pegboard on the back side of the pine boards you just installed, the doors will open farther, and you'll get another cool-looking dark strip resembling a walnut inlay **(Photo 4)**. Even with the filler strips, the cabinet doors will make contact with the wall about 4 in. before they fully open. If you really, really want the doors to open all the way, you can add another 1/4 in. of filler to the back. But if you hang tools on the front of the cabinet or on the walls on either side, it shouldn't matter at all.

## CUTTING LIST

| KEY | QTY. | SIZE & DESCRIPTION |
|---|---|---|
| A | 2 | 3-1/2" x 46-1/4" x 3/4" pine (base top/bottom) |
| B | 6 | 3-1/2" x 47-3/4" x 3/4" pine (base/door sides) |
| C | 4 | 3-1/2" x 22-1/4" x 3/4" pine (door tops/bottoms) |
| D | 2 | 3/4" x 40-3/4" x 3/4" pine (base side spacers) |
| E | 2 | 3-1/2" x 47-3/4" x 3/4" pine (base top/bottom spacer) |
| F | 1 | 3/4" x 40-3/4" x 3/4" pine (base center brace) |
| G | 4 | 3/4" x 22-1/4" x 3/4" pine (door top/bottom spacer) |
| H | 4 | 3/4" x 47-3/4" x 3/4" pine (door side spacer) |
| J | 1 | 48" x 48" x 1/4" pegboard (base pegboard); trim after attaching to frame |
| K | 4 | 48" x 24" x 1/4" pegboard* (door pegboards); trim after attaching to frame |
| L | 2 | 1" x 47-3/4" x 1/4" pegboard filler strips for base sides |
| M | 2 | 3-1/2" x 45-3/4" x 1/4" pegboard filler strips for base top and bottom |
| N | | 24' of screen mold; cut to fit |

*Or white gloss hardboard panel

## MATERIALS LIST

| ITEM | QTY. |
|---|---|
| 1x4 x 8' pine | 7 |
| 4' x 8' x 1/4" pegboard | 2 |
| 4' x 8' x 1/4" white/gloss hardboard panel | 1 |
| 1/4" x 3/4" x 8' screen mold | 3 |
| Wood glue, 4' piano hinges, magnet catches, 2" trim screws, 1-1/2" 18-gauge brads, 1" 18-gauge brads, 1 qt. of polyurethane | |

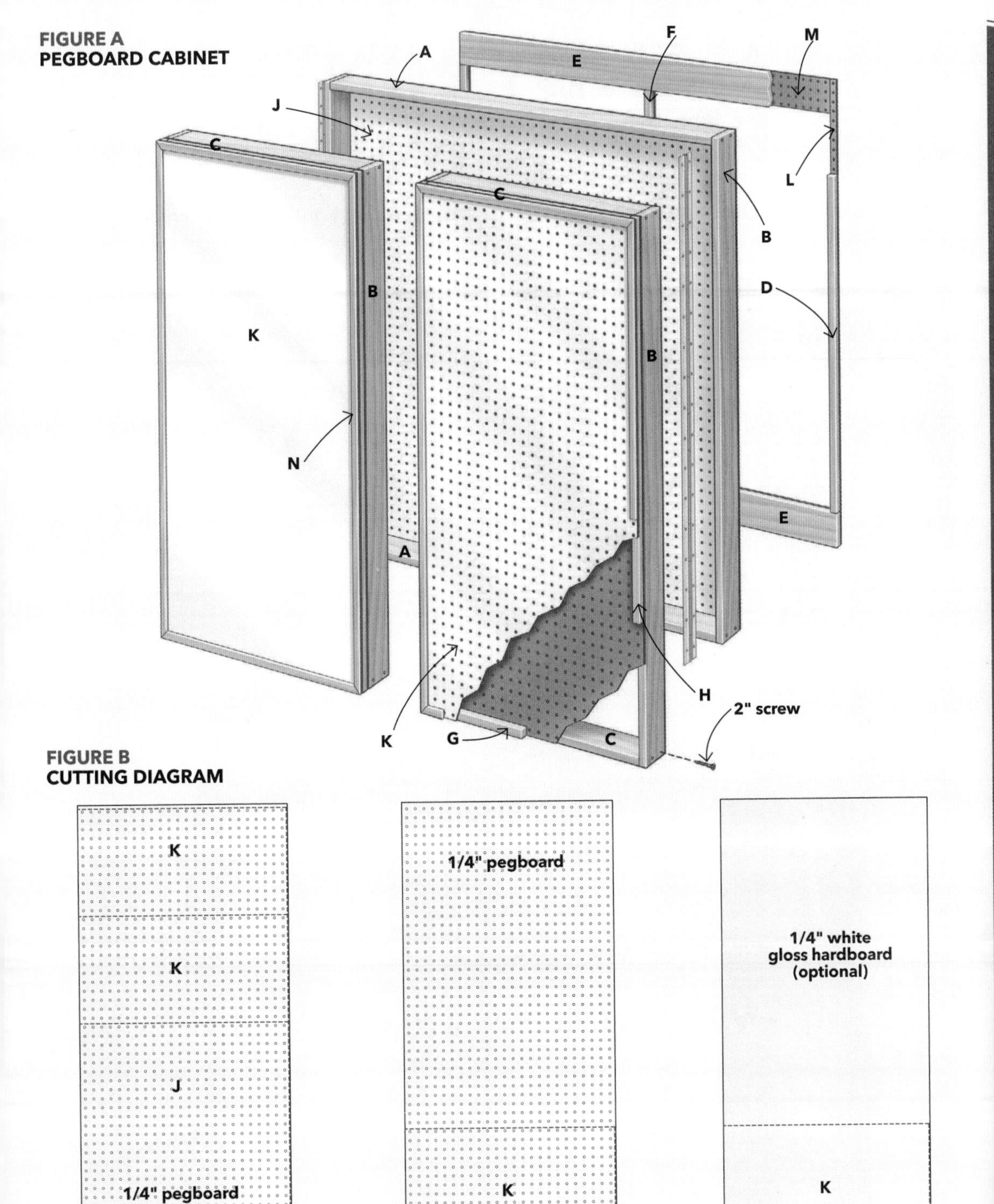
FIGURE A
PEGBOARD CABINET
A
E
F
M
J
C
L
C
B
B
D
K
B
N
E
A
H
2" screw
K
G
C
FIGURE B
CUTTING DIAGRAM
K
K
J
1/4" pegboard
1/4" pegboard
K
1/4" white
gloss hardboard
(optional)
K

# HANDY HINTS FOR PAINTING

**We have tips for everything, from touch-ups to gear organization.**

## ELEVATE, THEN PAINT

Ever paint a chair and have it stick to your newspaper or drop cloth? Paint hassle-free by driving drywall screws about 1/2 in. into the bottoms of the chair legs. Raising the chair this way makes it easier to paint and even lets you coat the bottoms of the legs. This works great with brush-on paint as well.

# Nail Hole Spot Marking

If you're painting a wall on which a lot of photos are hanging, don't be fearful. Instead of dreading how paint will hide the nail holes or fretting that it'll take forever to reestablish each photo's exact location, just stick a large-head pin into each nail hole. Then roll paint right over the pinheads. After the paint dries, pluck out the pins, replace the nails and hang your pictures right back up on the wall.

# Never Clean a Roller Tray

Instead of buying liners for your plastic paint roller tray, just let the paint dry and pour new paint right over it for the next job. When the paint starts getting thick, peel it out and throw it in the trash. You'll have one tray forever and probably won't need to buy another one.

# PAINTING GEAR ORGANIZER

It can be difficult to keep track of painting tools, and sometimes it seems as if you can never find what you need. To keep it all together, drill two holes in the side of a large plastic container and knot the ends of a bungee cord in the holes. Stand all your tools in between the cord and the side of the container. Now it'll be very easy to see everything you've got so you can grab exactly what you need.

## PIMPLE PADS FOR PAINT CLEANUP

Facial cleansing wipes aren't just for pimple prevention. The alcohol in the wipes softens latex paint but won't harm most surfaces (test first to make sure). They work best on paint that's been dry just a few hours.

# Clean Crusty Paintbrushes

After you paint with latex for a few hours, the brush gets a gummy, partially dry ring of paint near the top of the bristles. Instead of getting frustrated while trying to rub it away with your fingers, use a fingernail brush. Just wet the paintbrush with warm, soapy water, and scrub back and forth to loosen the gunk. Then use downward strokes to comb the paint from the bristles. This works wonderfully for hands, too.

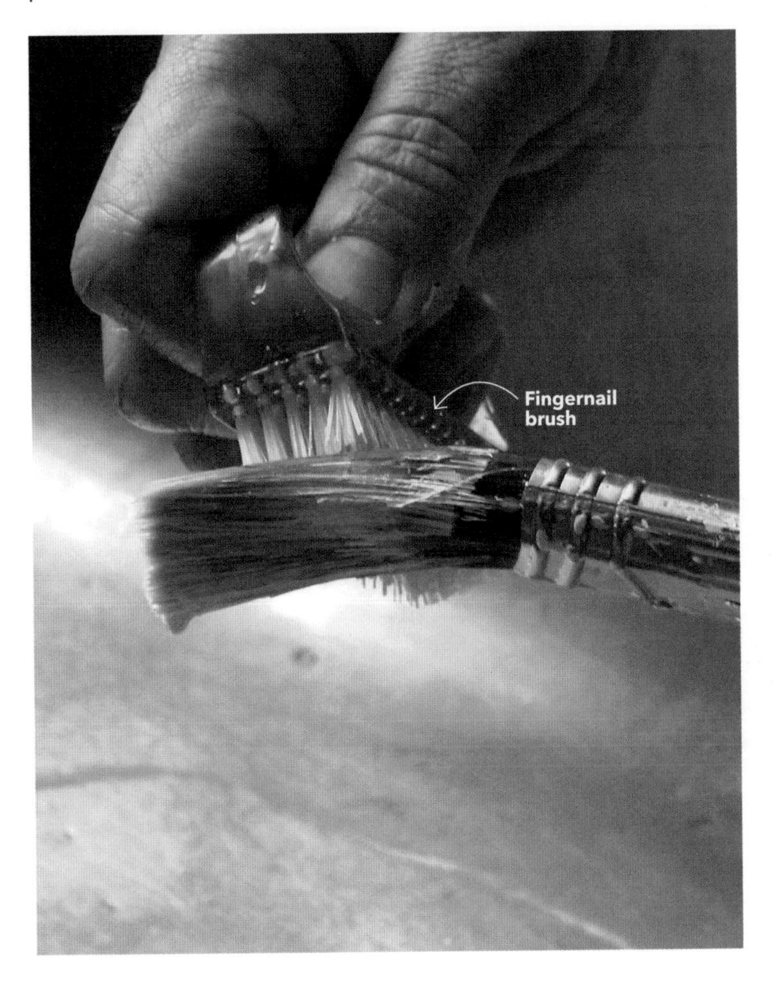

# Perfect Paint Touch-Ups

After certain jobs, like a kitchen cabinet remodel, you might find yourself constantly touching up paint here and there. Having to open a can of paint and clean brushes each time is a pain, but here's a slick solution: Clean out a bottle of nail polish using nail polish remover, fill it with the paint you used and put it in a kitchen drawer. Now small, quick touch-ups will be a breeze.

## NO-HASSLE PAINT TOUCH-UPS

No sooner do you finish painting a wall and cleaning up the rollers, brushes and putting away the gear than you find some spots that need touching up. Don't bother getting the tools dirty again. Instead of a roller, use an old washcloth or chunk of towel to do the job. Just ball up the washcloth, dip it in the paint can and bounce it over the spot a few times. The washcloth leaves the same kind of texture as a roller sleeve and you can throw it away when you're done. Zero cleanup!

## SPRAY-CLEAN ROLLER

Spin most of the excess paint off your roller sleeve by holding the roller frame inside a bucket and hitting the sleeve with the spray from a nozzled garden hose. In seconds it'll be nearly paint free. You will still have to use soap and water to finish the job, but this will give you a huge head start.

## Slick Corner Painting Tip

Here's a neat trick for painting corners where two different colors meet on adjoining walls. Instead of taping right at the corner, cheat the tape a quarter inch away from the corner and run it down the wall's nice flat surface. It's much easier to get the tape to look straight and you don't fight the corner. This works especially well when you're butting darker and lighter colors together.

# Give It the Brush-Off

Cleaning brushes, like cleaning the outdoor grill, is down there on most lists of chores. But there's a trick that makes the job a lot more palatable. If you run the brush under water before you start painting, the cleanup is a snap. Of course, this works only for latex paints, primers and finishes.

## KEEP RIM RUST OUT OF PAINT

You can get a clean pour out of an old paint can that has rust debris in its rim. Just wrap the rim with tape to seal in the debris while you pour.

## LADLE, NOT POUR

When you need a small amount of paint, don't pour it out of the can. Use a soup ladle! You won't mess up the can rim or slop paint down the side, and you can ladle out exactly what you need. Bon appetit!

# Pizza Box Spray Paint Booth

Here's a tip that really delivers: For small projects, build a spray paint booth from large pizza boxes. Raise the lids, tape them together at the seam to create a corner and begin painting. Be sure to wear a paint vapor mask.

CHAPTER 5

# EVERYDAY SOLUTIONS

BUY A TOOL KIT & GET TWO SELECT
POWER TOOLS OR BATTERIES
handyman
PRO
ENTER NOW
Justin Bieber & Selena Gomez
Getting Cozy Again

## MESSAGE BOARD DOOR

Entry doors with glass panes can be used as message centers. Just use a dry-erase marker to leave notes and reminders.

# Headache Remedy

Whenever you buy child-protected bottles of aspirin or ibuprofen, color both of the white arrows with red fingernail polish. That way, when you need some medicine, you can immediately see how the arrows line up and get the cap off quickly.

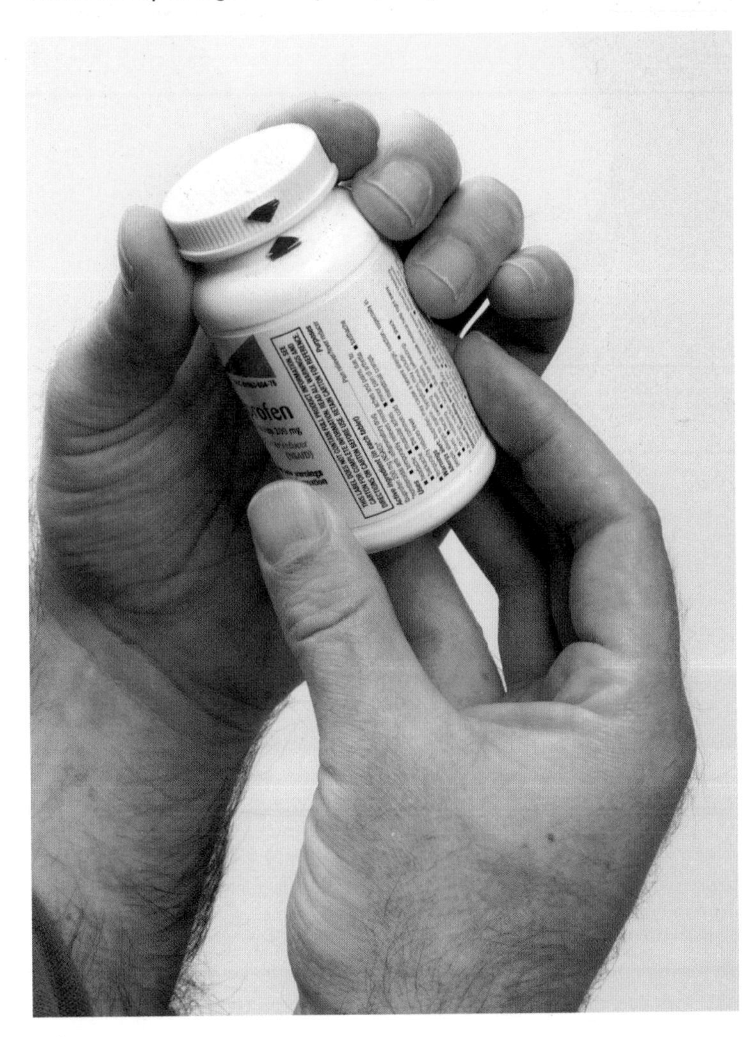

# Wider Flashlight Beam

When there's a power outage and it's suddenly dark, we all usually hunt for a flashlight. Such a light is helpful, but it is limited to a small concentrated beam. Make it more useful by broadening the beam of light with a rubber band, a clothespin and a white paper plate. The paper plate can be bent to spread the light over a larger area. This means you can still play cribbage while you're up at the cabin!

# SHOP VACUUM AIR MATTRESS PUMP

Holidays usually mean guests staying over, and blowing up inflatable air mattresses for guest beds can be a hassle. Next time company's coming, try this trick: Use your shop vacuum! It's simple to turn your machine into a temporary compressor. Just hook up the hose to the vacuum's exhaust port and hold the other end to the mattress's release valve. When you're ready to deflate the mattress, connect it to the suction port. Now it takes only a minute or two to fill and deflate a mattress.

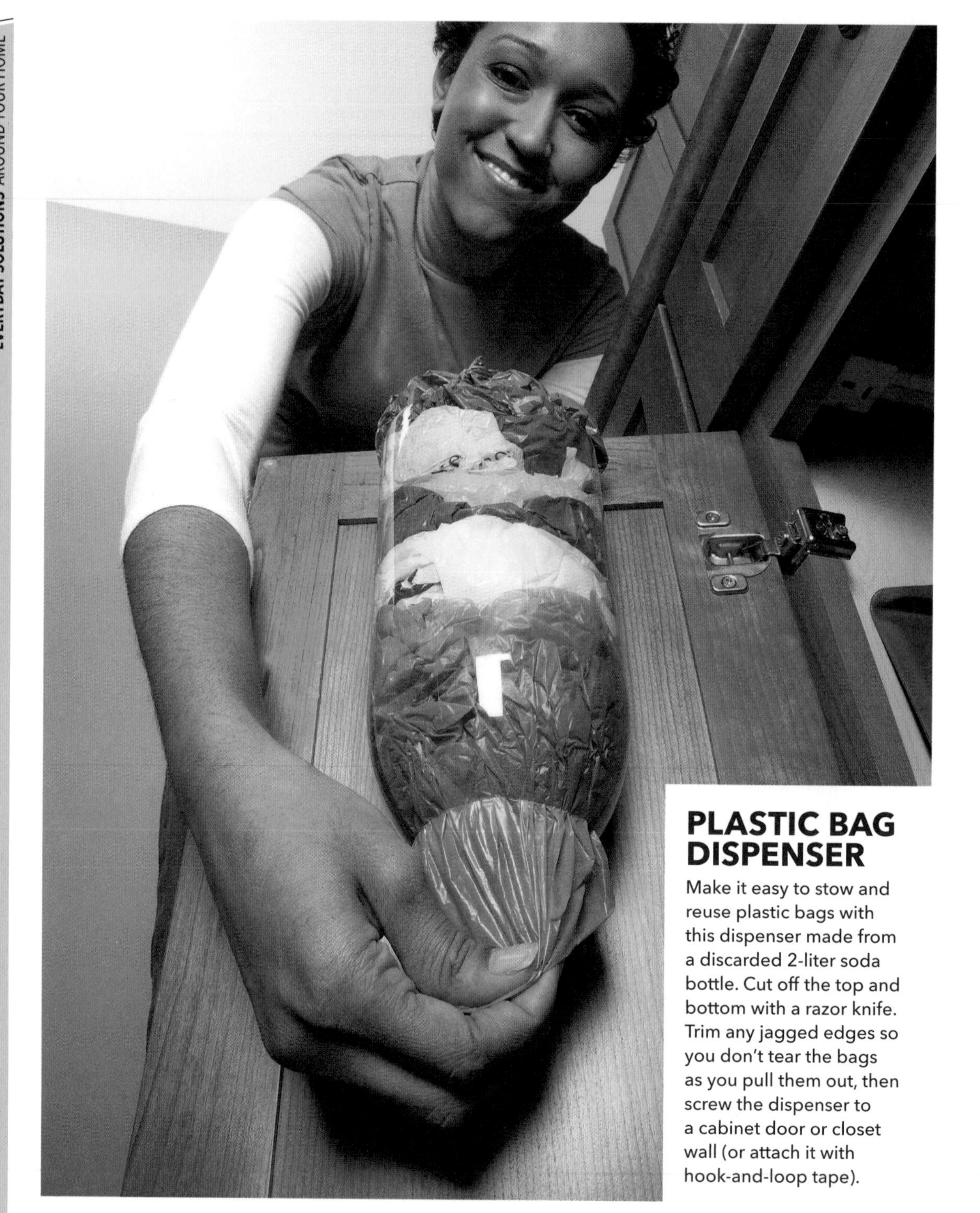

## PLASTIC BAG DISPENSER

Make it easy to stow and reuse plastic bags with this dispenser made from a discarded 2-liter soda bottle. Cut off the top and bottom with a razor knife. Trim any jagged edges so you don't tear the bags as you pull them out, then screw the dispenser to a cabinet door or closet wall (or attach it with hook-and-loop tape).

# Effortless Wrinkle Removal

Don't like ironing? Or often forget to take your clothes out of the dryer? No problem! To remove the wrinkles, throw a few ice cubes or a wet washcloth in with your dry clothes and run the dryer again for about 10 minutes. The added dampness steams out the wrinkles without effort on your part. This trick is most effective on lighter-weight fabrics.

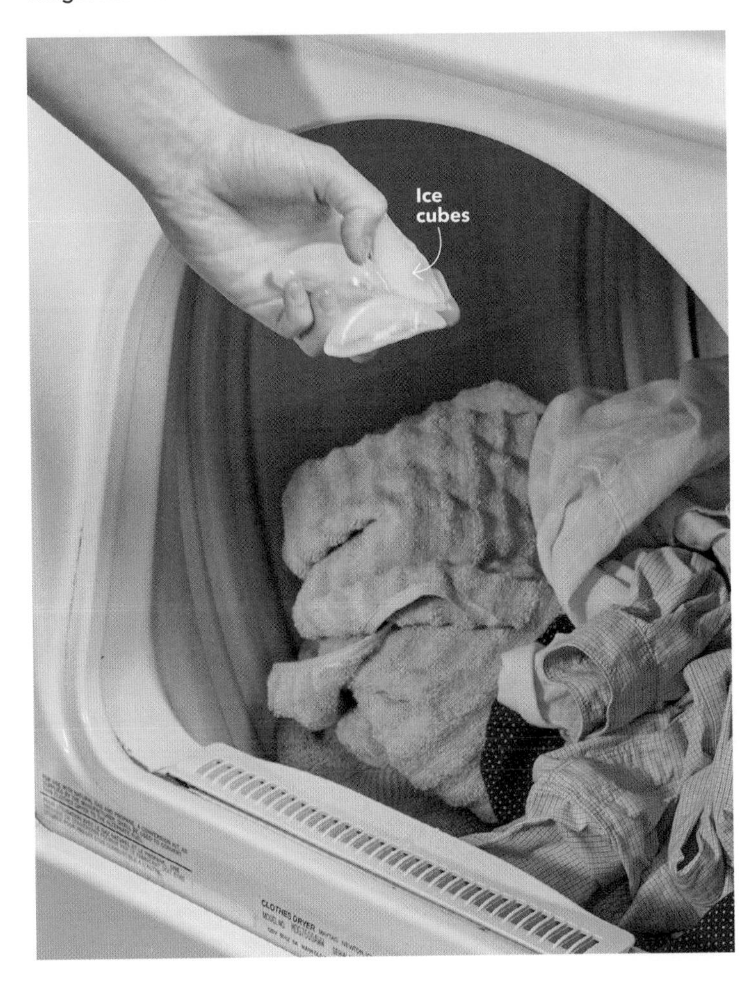

# No More Loose Screws

The tiny screws in your glasses can back themselves out over time. If you don't have a thread-locking product, try clear nail polish instead. Works like a charm!

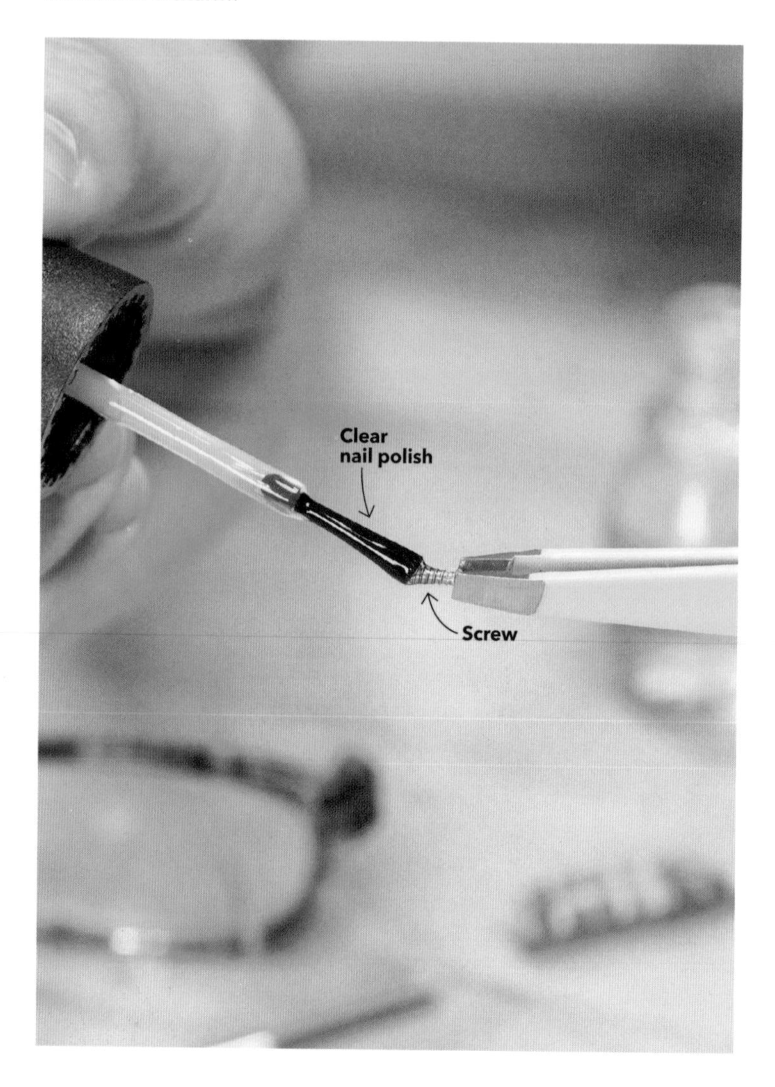

## TOTE BAG STIFFENER

Reusable grocery bags are easier to load if you add a little more structure. Just cut a piece of tempered hardboard or plywood to fit the bottom. You can also try inserting a cardboard box—maybe even make one to fit your bag perfectly.

# RECYCLED-DENIM APRON

Don't toss those worn-out jeans just yet—turn them into a gardening apron. Cut off the legs and the front, leaving the back and the waistband intact. Then slip on the apron, turn it around and load the pockets with tools.

## Loosen a Stuck Lid

Stubborn lids are no match for duct tape. Just wrap a piece around the lid, leaving a tail for a handle. Be sure the duct tape is fastened only to the lid, not the jar. Hold the jar with one hand and pull the handle with the other. If the jar is full of liquid, do this in the sink to avoid a mess.

# A Tougher Towel Rack

Tired of rambunctious kids yanking the towel rack off the wall? Cut a piece of oak a little longer than the mounting bracket spacing, rout the edges and finish it to match the bathroom trim. Then screw it to the wall studs and mount the towel bar to its new base. No matter how tough your kids are on that towel rack, it'll hold fast.

## LONG-REACH BUG GRABBER

It always seems as if bugs show up on the ceiling, where it's often tough to reach them. This handy-dandy bug grabber, made from an old foam mop and some duct tape, solves that problem with ease. Just wrap the mop head with duct tape, sticky side out, and you'll be armed and dangerous. You can reach any critter high on the wall or ceiling and stick it to the tape. When the mop loses its "grab," just wrap on another layer.

# Simple Computer Shelf

To get your laptop at a comfy height for working, make this shelf for your desk with some leftover boards, glue and a few finish nails. You can use a 12-in. x 24-in. piece of plywood for the platform and two 12-in. pieces of 1x3 for the supports. Attach the supports with glue and finish nails or screws. The open space is a good spot to stash a pad of paper, books or a keyboard when it's not in use.

## INSERT A KEY, OPEN A BOTTLE

Got a wine bottle that just won't open? Push a key into the cork at a 45-degree angle until the key's teeth are all the way in the cork. Then twist and pull the cork up and out.

## FREE CHIP CLIPS

Who likes to spend money on items when you can get them for free? When you get clothes hangers with plastic clips from clothing bought at department stores, cut off the ends and use the clips to keep bags of chips fresh.

# Magic Label Remover

When you buy new plastic food storage containers, the gummed label always turns into a gooey, smeared mess when you try to peel it off. You can scrub, scrape and soak it, but there always seems to be a little adhesive left behind. Here's a simple trick: Fill the container with hot tap water, but keep the label dry. Let it sit for a few minutes to soften the adhesive, and then slowly peel off the label. Voilà! A perfectly clean plastic container.

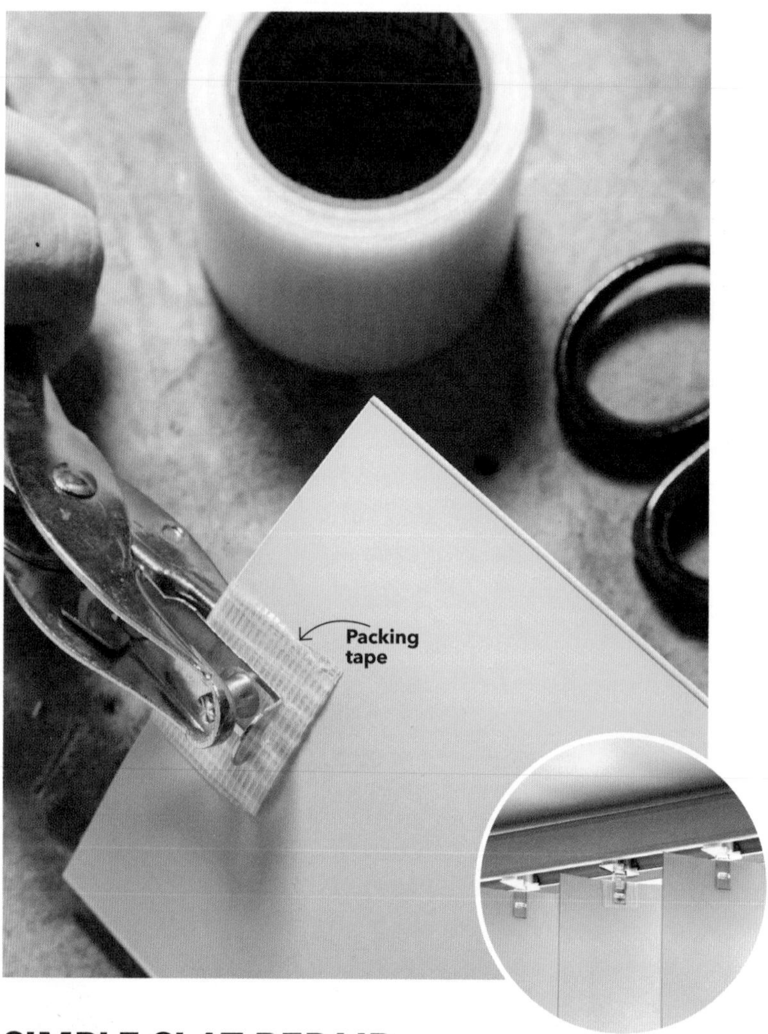


## SIMPLE SLAT REPAIR

Here's a quick and easy way to fix a broken slat in your vertical blinds. Cover the broken area with two layers of packing tape. Use a hole punch to make a new hole for the clip. Clip the slat into place, and move on to your next project!

# No-Spill Grocery Bags

It's a pain to crawl deep into the trunk to get all the groceries that have spilled out of your bags on the way home from the store. Here's an effective solution: Run a long bungee cord through the bag handles and hook the ends to the sides of the trunk. Keep the bungee cord in the trunk so it's there when you need it.

# Trash Can Hauler

For folks who have a long driveway and a bad back, hauling the trash out to the street can be a pain. Make it easy by using your noggin and your tractor. On trash days, just get on the tractor, grab onto the can and roll it down the driveway.

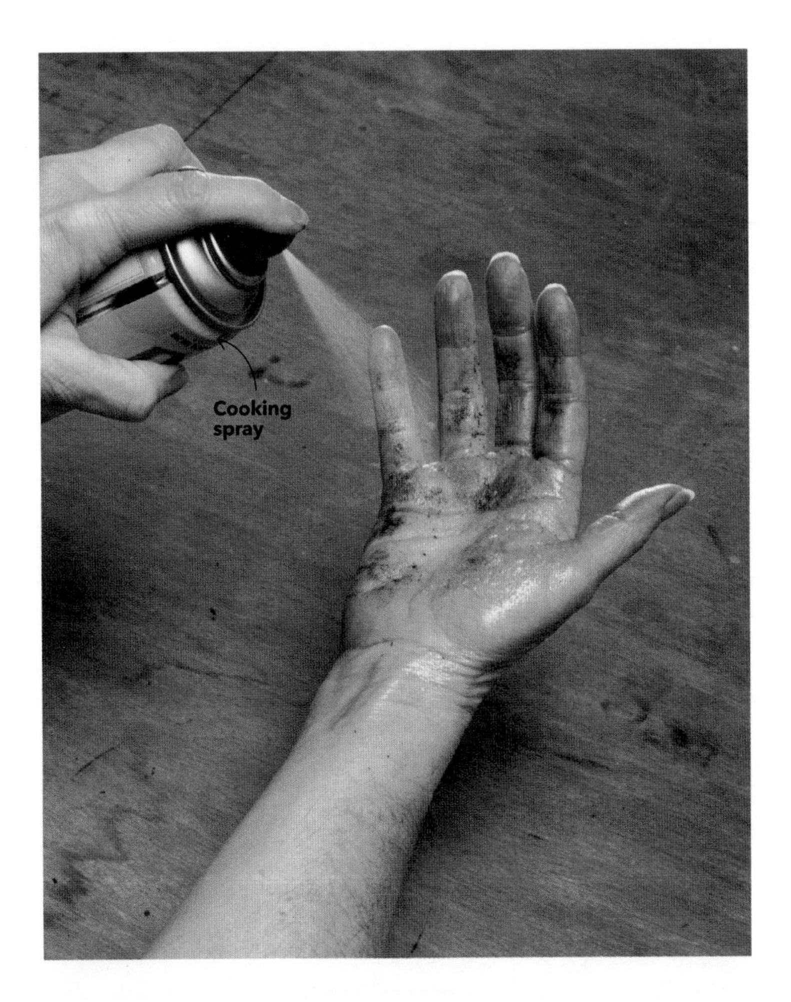


# SIMPLE SAP REMOVER

Tree sap on garden hoses can make for a tricky, sticky mess. Trying to get the sap off your hands every time you water is a pain—unless you try this easy trick: Use cooking spray. Just a small squirt and a quick wipe with a paper towel is all it takes to get the stuff off. You might even want to keep a can of cooking spray in your garage, since the spray removes most oil-based paints and primers, too.

## OUTLET STRIP PROTECTOR

If you do a lot of power sanding at your workbench, the sawdust can work its way into the outlet strip and interfere with the electrical contact. Just put a strip of masking tape over the outlets you're not using, and replace it as needed. The outlet strip will last a lot longer!

# Weed ID

Each spring, many gardeners battle pesky weeds with a spray bottle of herbicide. But it's hard to tell which weeds were sprayed and which ones you missed. Try mixing a tiny amount of red food coloring into the herbicide. Now when you spray those evil creatures, you can see their "wounds" and know you've hit them where it hurts. You'll save time and money, and it'll give you hope that you might win the war against all that creeping Charlie!

# High-Visibility Boundary Marker

Each year, it's a good idea to mark the boundaries of your yard so the snowplow driver doesn't inadvertently damage your lawn. Rebar along the perimeter is one option, but the driver isn't always able to see it at night. Here's a better solution: Slip a brightly colored swim noodle over each rebar. No one can miss those markers now!

# DUCT TAPE DRINK HOLDER

Keep a roll of duct tape on the center floorboard in your truck. It works great as a cup holder, and it's sticky enough to stay put. Plus, when you end up needing the roll, you'll know right where to find it.

## HIGH-RISE BIRD FEEDER

Deer, unfortunately, can enjoy seed just as much as birds do. To keep the food for your feathered friends away from the deer, drive a steel stake into the ground and attach an extendable painter's pole to the stake. Then attach the bird feeder to the other end. Now you can lower the bird feeder to fill it and then raise it to keep the seed "for birds only."

# Keep Your Camping Gear Dry

To help keep your clothes and supplies dry, line your camping bag with a plastic garbage bag before packing. Then close the garbage bag with a twist tie.

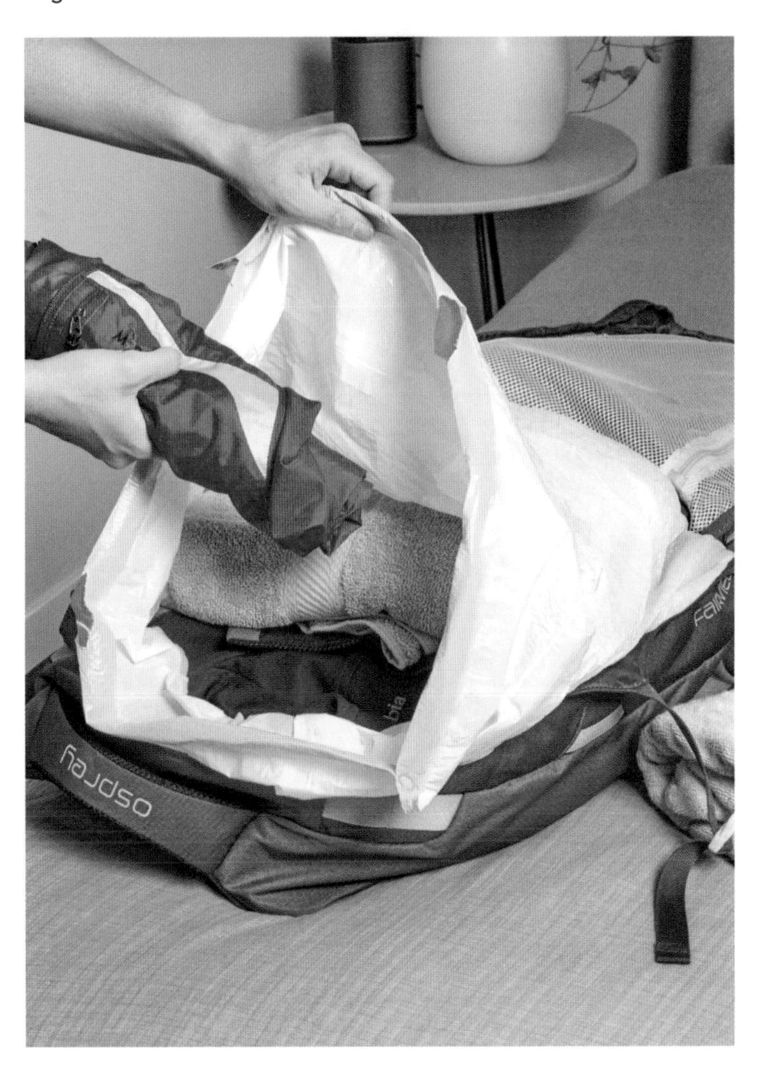

# Permanent Tiki Torch Holders

Tiki torches are always fun decorations, but when the ground is hard, it's not easy to push them in—or to remove them every time you mow. For a solution, cut 5-in.-long pieces of PVC pipe to hold the torches, and use a maul and a block of wood to pound each one into the ground. (You might have to pull each one out a couple of times during the process to dig out the clay plugs.) Now you can slip the torches in and out of their sleeves, and mow right over the PVC.

# DOG DETANGLER

Stop the game of tug-of-war between your dog's tie-out cable and your deck boards. Tack down an inexpensive plastic corner protector with galvanized finishing nails to keep Bingo's line from getting stuck in the gaps between the boards.

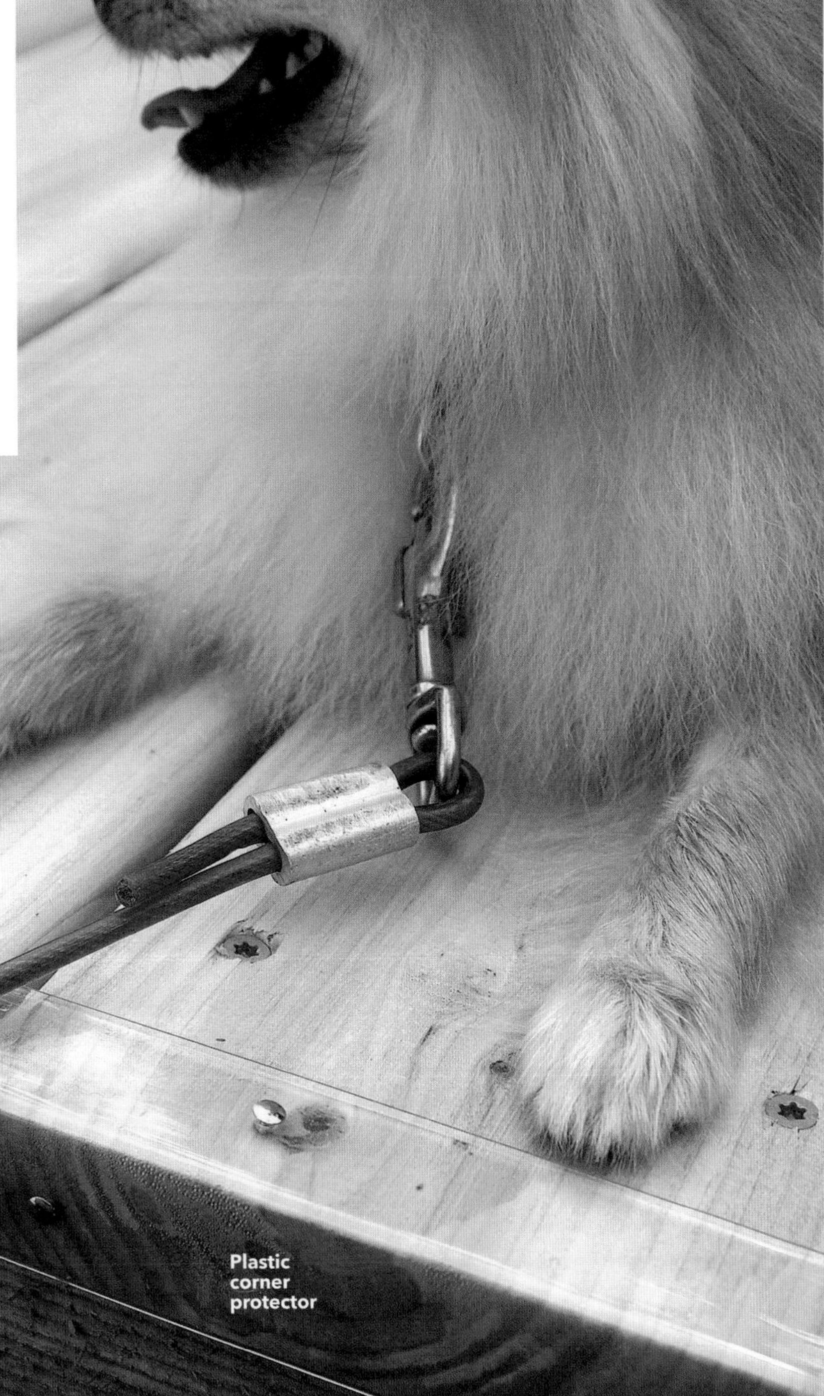

## POOP PIPE

You and your dogs have an arrangement: They poop; you pick it up. But rather than make daily trips to the trash can, build this poop pipe. It's just a large piece of 4-in. PVC drainpipe sunk into the ground a foot or so, with a trash bag lining and a cap sitting loosely on top. A rubber band holds the bag in place, and the cap helps keep odors at bay. When the bag gets full, just take it to the trash bin and put a new bag in the drainpipe.

# Chimney Flue Planters

To make these terra-cotta planters, go to a brick supplier and buy 3-ft. lengths of clay chimney flue liner. Cut them to different heights using a circular saw fitted with an abrasive cutting wheel. You can put them on a deck or patio, or accent your yard wherever you'd like—just pick your spots and bury the ends in the soil a little. Fill the liners with gravel for drainage, leaving 8 in. at the top for potting soil. (Since the water can drain, the liners won't crack if they freeze.) Or just set pots on top of the gravel and bring in the plants for the winter.

# Easy-To-Remove Garbage Bags

Getting a full trash bag out of the can is always a bear because of the vacuum seal that forms between the bag and the can. Solve the problem by drilling holes in the side of the garbage can near the bottom. Air is allowed into the bottom of the can when you pull out the bag, so the bag slides out with ease.

## NO-SLIDE LAUNDRY LINE

Tired of hanging your clothes on the line and having all the hangers slide to the center? Use plastic chain instead. No more sliding, and the links separate the clothes so they dry quicker. This solution works perfectly in the laundry room or outside in the yard!

## SPRING SLEDDING

A plastic snow sled is useful in the off-season, too. Use it to haul yard debris, bags of concrete and plants. The sled slides over grass, sand and gravel with ease. You can even use it to haul camping gear from the car to the campsite—amazing!

## A Movable Feast

Late frosts in spring and early frosts in fall can kill your tender veggies and herbs. Extend the gardening season by planting them in a shallow wheelbarrow. Wheel your small crop around to follow the sun, shade or rain, and when the weather threatens to turn cold overnight, just roll your portable garden into the garage for protection.

## Decorate a Lamppost

You can train an annual like morning glory or hyacinth bean vine to crawl up a handsome boulevard lamppost or lawn light. Wrap the post with chicken wire and then plant seeds (or seedlings you started indoors) at the base of the lamppost each spring. By midsummer, the vine will encircle the lamppost. By August, it will reach the top and be in full flower.

# LIGHTWEIGHT PLANT CONTAINERS

Large plant containers can be too heavy to move once you've filled them with plants and soil. Lighten the load and save on potting mix by partially filling a pot with expanding foam insulation (Dow Great Stuff Window and Door works well). Just wrap waxed paper around a paper towel core and hold it over the drainage hole. Fill the pot about a third full with the foam insulation. It works best to fill it in a few layers, letting each layer harden before adding the next. (Otherwise, the foam near the bottom stays gooey for days.) Then remove the paper towel core. Make sure you screen the drainage hole when you pour in your soil so your pot is able to drain well.

# HANDY HINTS FOR YOUR CAR

**Tips to help you remove bumper stickers, protect doors and more.**

## TIRE CHAIN GANG

Snow blower chains pop off when you least expect it. Here's a simple solution that will prevent the chain from unhooking and coming loose. Tie the locking links in place with nylon zip ties. The chains will stay secure until you decide it's time to take them off.

## Easy-To-Check Dipstick

When changing the oil on a lawn mower, the oil and the dipstick are often so clean that it's hard to check the level. Mark the low line of the dipstick with a permanent marker to make it much easier to read.

# Truck-Bed Caddy

Pickup trucks are fantastic for hauling big stuff, but small stuff has a way of sliding all over the place. To solve the problem, make a simple caddy from 2x4s and fasten it with deck screws. The compartments help small items like nursery plants stay put.

## STREAK-FREE CAR

Your car will look as if it rolled out of a professional car wash when you dry it with your leaf blower. Blow away the bulk of the water with the leaf blower and then finish up with a quick towel swipe. You'll have a streak-free finish without a pile of wet towels and no waiting around to start waxing.

## HIGH-VISIBILITY TRAILER

Paint the top of your trailer's loading ramp white so you can see it better. It makes a huge difference when backing up, especially on rainy days. At night, your reverse lights will reflect off the white paint so you can maneuver the trailer much more easily.

## Boat Trailer Guides

Depending on what kind of truck you have, it can be tough to see your boat trailer behind the truck when the boat isn't on it, which makes backing up the empty trailer really difficult. But there's an easy solution: Install two fiberglass driveway markers on the trailer with hose clamps. You'll easily see where the back of the empty trailer is, and the guides will help you center the boat on the trailer when loading it.

# Handy Paper Towel Holder

Attach a roll of paper towels to the inside of your car trunk lid with a short bungee cord. The towels will be handy when you need them but won't take up space (or get wrecked) rolling around your trunk.

## REMOVABLE BUMPER STICKERS

Bumper stickers are frequently very hard to remove—but they don't have to be. Cut magnetic vent covers the same size as your bumper stickers. Stick a bumper sticker to a vent cover and attach the magnetic side to your car. Presto: removable bumper stickers! Magnetic sheets are handy for hanging decorations on the fridge, too.

# CARDBOARD DROP CLOTH

Most cardboard boxes end up in the recycling bin, but make sure to save a couple of the larger ones. They're perfect for keeping your clothes clean when you crawl under the car. And there's no need to worry about clutter; stored flat, they don't take up much room.

# Lighted Floor Jack

Positioning a jack in the right place under a car usually requires a shop light. Simplify the operation by attaching a battery-powered self-adhesive LED puck light to the base of the jack. Now you can just turn on the light, roll the jack under the car in exactly the right spot and get to work. LED puck lights are available at most hardware stores and home centers.

## Car Door Protector

Here's a way to prevent dings in your car doors and dents in your finished garage walls. Use a pool noodle toy instead of a regular door guard. Just make a slit in the noodle with a utility knife, run a bungee cord or a rope through the middle, and attach it to screw eyes on the garage wall. Now that's using your noodle!